CHANNELING JESUS AND THE HOLY SPIRITS

BARRY R. STROHM

Published by
Hybrid Global Publishing
301 East 57th Street
4th Floor
New York, NY 10022

Manufactured in the United States of America, or in the United Kingdom when distributed elsewhere.

Strohm, Barry R.
Spirits Speak: Channeling Jesus and the Holy Spirits
LCCN: 2020914941

ISBN: 978-1-951943-31-8
eBook: 978-1-951943-32-5

Cover design by: Jonathan Pleska
Copyediting by: Lara Kennedy
Author photo by: Nicole Daacke
Interior Design by: Suba Murugan

www.wordsofgodthenandnow.com

www.spiritspredict.com

DEDICATION

First of all, I would like to dedicate this book to all of the incredible holy spirits that came forward to our channeling sessions and gave us the messages and information about their lives found in this book. This is their work, and Connie and I are simply bearers of their words. We are humbled that she and I have been chosen for this mission. Our hope is that we have lived up to their expectations.

My wife, Connie, has been at my side throughout the process of receiving and writing the words of the holy spirits. Her soul is a shining light as she works as an inspiration to others. My soul was truly blessed when she was selected to return and become my partner and the love of my life. As we grow old together, I know that this journey is nearing its end. My hope is that we will be able to return many more times and work as a team to spread the loving words of our Lord. Without her, none of this would be possible.

EPIGRAPH

Know I am always with you. There are times that you will doubt my presence, but I am still with you. Have faith, and all will be fine. Do not fear; I am with you. Have love in your hearts and love God.

PREFACE

Many speak to God every day in prayer, but very few hear his actual words in return. Throughout the ages, a few individuals have been given the gift of prophecy and the ability to speak the words of Jesus and the holy spirits. The author is one of those individuals. The reader can decide for themselves if the messages are actually the words of the holiest of spirits and, in some instances, the words of Jesus, or the universal energy of God.

In this book, you can read the channeled words of:

- The prophet Moses
- John the Baptist
- Andrew the Disciple
- Mary Magdalene
- Simon Peter
- Saint Matthew
- Saint Timothy
- Saint Thomas
- Paul the Apostle
- Toba, the wife of Jesus
- Blessed Mother Mary
- Messages of Jesus
- Constantine the Great
- Saint Augustine

- Mother Teresa
- Reverend Billy Graham

In this book, you will participate in the modern miracle of reading the contemporary words of the holiest of spirits telling of their lives, deaths, and messages of inspiration for all. Much of the information is unique and has never been in print before. Some of the information will differ from the classical teachings of organized religions. You will learn of the many paths to the realms of heaven based on a unifying message of love for all. Approach this book with an open mind and enjoy the truth concerning the journey of the soul, both during incarnate lives and after the passing of the soul upon physical death.

Since no one really knows the true appearance of Jesus and his followers, I decided to include images created in oil by the old master painters. These artists used the early gospels as guides in creating their masterpieces that, in their minds, fulfilled the images depicted in the Bible. As you will see, many of them do not duplicate the facts told to us by Jesus and the saints. I hope you enjoy viewing these famous images.

ACKNOWLEDGMENTS

We began our journey of learning to communicate with the spirit world in Salt Lake City, Utah. It is there that we were introduced to a special channeling board by K and Doc Kivett, along with Sammi Tall. The channeling board they used was designed by Sam and Carol Green and had been used by their family for two generations. Their patience was instrumental in Connie's and my learning how to use the board and receive our messages. We also welcome the occasional appearance of Carol Green since her passing.

I would like to send a special thank-you to Doris Siefker. She is a member of our Facebook group, Words of God Then and Now, and has performed an invaluable service. Whenever we do a live channeling session, she transcribes the words and sends them to me the next morning. Her work has saved me a huge amount of time, and we thank her.

CONTENTS

CHAPTER 1

Personal Journey

In my earlier books, I laid the foundation for understanding the life and words of the Lord. In *Spirits Speak of the Universe*, I devoted chapters to the Universal God and universal reincarnation. My last book, *Spirits Speak: Channeling the Life of Jesus*, told of information we channeled about the missing 28 years in the life of Jesus, as well as information about his disciples and followers. That book laid the foundation for the words that are presented in this volume. In that book, you learned that Jesus lived a relatively normal life until he began his ministries. That life included a wife and five children. It also stressed his relatively simple message of love and living a good life so your soul can advance in heaven as it becomes more like God. Here, we will expand on his words by bringing you the messages of Jesus and those of the disciples, followers, and servants.

There are many individuals and books that claim they speak or contain the words of God. In this book, we take a very unique approach, in that you can go to my YouTube channel and watch the videos of our channeling sessions with our Lord and the holiest of spirits. You can watch the videos, hear the words as we received them, and make up your own mind. You can also go to my website, www.wordsofgodthenandnow.com, and read the raw transcripts of the words as we received them. I have absolutely no doubts that we are bringing you the words of Jesus, the saints, and the holy spirits. Our intent in this book is not to undermine the Bible or organized religions but to bring you truths about the life of Jesus, his followers, and his words. You will see that the messages are beautiful and will instill a fresh love for God. We hope this book will contribute to giving you understanding as to the complex journey your soul goes through to advance in the realms of heaven. It will also tell you of the perils the soul faces because of free will and ego.

If someone told me 20 years ago that I would be communicating with Jesus and the holiest of spirits, I would have told them they were crazy. At that time, even though I was spiritual, I did not even believe in ghosts and made fun of anyone that would tell stories like what is happening to us today. Having a business management degree and a civil engineering license, I worked in the construction and stone quarry business all my life. At one point in my life, I was CEO of a group of stone quarries. This is not exactly a background conducive to spirituality and communication with the holiest of spirits.

My wife, Connie, and I were always spiritual. We believed in the existence of God or a higher spiritual being. As a young child born in rural Pennsylvania, I attended an extremely strict church closely related to the Mennonite faith and even attended tent revivals with my grandmother. I tried reading the Bible but must admit to having a hard time understanding many of the verses. We tried to raise our two daughters in a spiritual environment and attended a Presbyterian church on a fairly regular basis. I was never completely satisfied with much that I was being told and slowly drifted away from church, but not my belief in a higher deity.

My personal and spiritual stories are told in previous books, especially *Afterlife: What Really Happens on the Other Side*, so I will not repeat myself here. Suffice it to say that my spirit guides led Connie and me along a path of learning that would allow us to communicate with the guides and spirits to provide the information included in this book. There were times that I found the information we were receiving to be unbelievable. My scientific background would kick in, requiring solid proof of what we were being told. When you are dealing with spirituality, solid proof is often hard to find. Faith is often the answer.

It has been a long journey from managing stone quarries to writing the contemporary messages of our Lord. Many of you will still be very skeptical, and rightly so. There have been many others that profess to have conversations with God. As you read the messages and words, I think you will come to realize that we are really bringing you his messages and advice for the evolution of humans on Earth. In my previous book, Spirits Speak: Channeling the Life of Jesus, we told the reader he lived a normal life, complete with a wife and five children, until starting his ministries at the age of 28. In this book, we bring you his messages, his answers to questions, and the stories of his apostles and holy spirits. Approach this book with an open mind and listen to the words of the holiest of spirits. Their messages are ones of love and compassion. Some of what you will read is in stark contrast to classic religious beliefs.

Our journey into the spirit world began when I purchased a haunted antique gallery in Pennsylvania 30 years ago but took a giant step forward in 2008, when economic conditions forced me to return to the store full-time. This event allowed the ghosts to introduce themselves, and I became obsessed with learning as much as possible about the other side. Another major event occurred when I was introduced to board channeling by friends in Salt Lake City, Utah. Board channeling provided the means to communicate with the spirit world and record their responses.

Communicating with a Spirit Board

For those of you not familiar with board channeling, we used a circular board, 20" x 20", with the letters and numbers in a circle around the outside of the board. There is a glass surface that protects the board from wear, and we use a shot glass in the place of a planchette. Connie and I would each put our fingers on the glass, and it was moved to the letters by spirit energy. The design of the board was given to us by the spirit guides during a channeling session. The guides also gave us this prayer of protection that we use when we begin a session:

> *God, please grant us your wisdom and protection. Grant us the knowledge that we can handle and keep us safe from all things that will harm us. Keep the messages*

positive and pure love. Keep us safe from our own ego. We ask these things in the light of the seen, the unseen, and the honesty of God.

Our Channeling Board – Barry Strohm

As Connie's and my psychic abilities improved, we became able to communicate with our spirit guides without any assistance from other psychics or even using the spirit board. Eventually, we were able to receive our messages mentally. As you watch the videos on my YouTube channel, you can watch as our abilities increase through the years. At this point of our education, we began to get personal messages from the holiest of spirits. Their messages began to indicate that we were on an incredibly special mission: to tell the true story of Jesus and his apostles. Needless to say, it took a bit of time for the impact of what we were doing to sink in. The first time Jesus came through for us, we were overcome by his wonderful energy. His words convinced us that we were truly communicating with the holiest of spirits.

A Special Mission from God

One thing we have learned in communicating with spirits is that all souls are members of soul families. Souls have reincarnated with members of their family many times. For instance, Connie and I have lived six or seven lifetimes together. We have been husband and wife, brother and sister, and in other relationships. Souls stick together on the other side and make plans to come back together. We were amazed to learn that God has a soul family and we were members of that soul family. Connie and I had been sent back to bring everyone the contemporary words of our Lord. We were told that much of what was written about him in the Bible was manipulated to strengthen the powers of man. He felt it was time for the truth to be told, and Connie and I were among those chosen to speak his words.

You can imagine how hard it was for a person that for 60 years of his life did not even believe in ghosts to understand that he was chosen to tell others the messages of Jesus and his apostles! In the beginning, I kept asking for some type of confirmation, and the different guides would confirm that the information was true. The challenge became how would I ever convince others that I was truly speaking the words of God? He not only convinced us that we were talking with our Lord, but he showed me how I would be able to convince skeptics in the future. As proof, Jesus gave me the power to heal others, much like he healed people when he walked the earth. He gave me a simple prayer that would direct the healing powers of God.

As proof of what he told me, one evening he came through and asked if I was ready to try healing others. I was scheduled to speak at a convention in Salt Lake City, and he gave me the name of a person to pray for that needed healing. When Jesus specifically asks you to do something, you do it. When I arrived at the convention, I became aware of a woman that was telling a friend about her chronic migraine headaches and that she was having one that was interfering with her ability to help at the convention. She gave me a very strange look when I asked her permission to pray for her and try to heal her headache. Approval was given, and I said the prayer as it was given to me. Within the hour, her headache was gone, and as I write this chapter, over one year later, she has suffered no more headaches. God healed her! Since that time, I have healed others, using the prayer that directs the healing power of God. Just as Jesus used his healing powers to show the people 2,000 years ago the power of the one God, he has chosen to give me a similar ability to prove to people that I am speaking and writing his words.

This book is the culmination of what Jesus has asked of us. We are presenting his messages on a wide variety of subjects. There are also chapters from channeling sessions with his mother, Mary, and his apostles, disciples, and other members of his soul family. They also bring words of love and understanding. Many of the subjects we cover in this book are very controversial, such as abortion and what is happening to our country. I am simply the messenger in bringing the reader the Lord's responses. His overriding message is of a simple love for one another and living a good life that will assist your soul in rising within the realms of heaven. His hope is that this book will become a guide for living your life and influencing others through his love and that of the holy spirits.

CHAPTER 2

Eternal Life, Reincarnation, and the Holy Soul Family

Have you ever wondered what Jesus really meant when he talked about everlasting life? I assume it is something everyone would like, but what is the true answer to how to obtain it? There are many verses in the New International Version of the Bible that refer to eternal or everlasting life. For instance:

John 3:16 – For God so loved the world, that he gave his only Son, that whoever believes in him should not perish but have eternal life.

John 6:40 – For this is the will of my Father, that everyone who looks on the Son and believes in him should have eternal life, and I will raise him on the last day.

Romans 6:23 – For the wages of sin is death, but the free gift of God is eternal life in Christ Jesus our Lord.

John 5:24 – Truly, truly I say to you, whoever hears my word and believes him who sent me has eternal life. He does not come into judgment, but has passed from death to life.

Matthew 25:46 – And these will go away into eternal punishment, but the righteous into eternal life.

John 3:36 – Whoever believes in the Son has eternal life; whoever does not obey the Son shall not see life, but the wrath of God remains on him.

There are many more verses, but you can see the general concept is that if you believe in God, you will enjoy eternal life in heaven. All of the verses indicate that you only have one lifetime to get it right. They also hint at the idea that if you do not get it right in that lifetime, you are going to face some type of eternal damnation. This introduction of fear is how the preaching of the love of God got subverted into fearing the wrath of God.

Reincarnation

In my previous books, I wrote extensively about reincarnation, or the ability of the soul energy to return for multiple lifetimes, so I will only make a few comments about it in this volume. We are told that soul energy dates to creation and that such energy can be neither created nor destroyed. Our scientists tell us that the creation of our universe took place over 13 billion years ago. That is a long time ago, especially when you consider that humans have only walked on our planet for around 250,000 years. If you look at that as a percentage of how long humans have been around compared to creation, the answer would be 0.00001923 percent. By any standards, that is insignificant.

The question becomes, then, where was all the soul energy before humans made their appearance on this planet? Soul energies were on other planets that had intelligent life during that time. Many were serving God on those planets and were rewarded by advancing in the realms of heaven. A human life is but a blink of an eye when compared to the number of incarnate lifetimes a soul energy has experienced. When Jesus spoke of eternal life, he was speaking of the eternal life of the soul energies, both as living incarnate and as spirit lives in heaven.

You will learn that Jesus spoke of reincarnation to his followers and disciples. He did not speak of it to the common person, because he considered it too difficult a concept for them to understand, and most of the individuals blessed to hear his words were uneducated and poor. He basically just told them that if they loved God, they would join him in heaven. By the middle of the fourth century, the Romans had outlawed the teaching of reincarnation, with the penalty of death, as the Roman Catholic Church became the official spokesman for God. Many of the gospels that spoke of reincarnation were destroyed.

About this time, the church fathers realized that they could better control their followers if they believed their souls only had one chance or lifetime to get it right and go to heaven. If they did not listen to the church, their souls would be sent to the eternal damnation of fire and brimstone in hell. Reincarnation gave the soul a little wiggle room, and that was not a good thing in the eyes of the church fathers. The wrath of God was to be feared, and the only path to salvation ran through the Catholic Church.

Many of us know of our prior lives and can prove it. In one of my immediate prior lives, I was a Confederate soldier who fought at the Battle of Gettysburg. I can go onto the battlefield at the location where I fought and communicate with the soldier with whom I fought over 150 years ago. Reincarnation is very real and the cornerstone for the advancement of the energy of the soul.

The Soul Family of God

Soul energies have had the opportunity to serve God since the beginning of time. The ones that have used their free will to serve him faithfully have ascended to the upper level, where they continue to serve. All the soul energies channeled in this book are members of the soul family of God. They have been sent to this and other planets many times to live incarnate lives in the service of God.

Throughout the history of the soul, God has guided many cultures in other worlds to show universal love and get along with each other. As I have written in my other books, there are advanced cultures on other planets that have learned the lesson of love and have progressed to the point where they live peacefully. This is obviously a lesson that still must be learned by humans. When God appeared to those other worlds and led them toward love and peaceful coexistence, he was assisted by other souls that worked with him, much like his disciples and followers when he walked the earth. The souls that assisted him in those other worlds progressed through the realms of heaven and became the soul family of God.

Those souls that are members of his soul family are selected to return to incarnate lives and assist others to learn the lessons of love so that they can progress through the realms as well. As you read each chapter of this book, you will see that the holy spirits have served God many times through uncountable different lifetimes. For instance, you will see that the soul of John the Baptist was Elijah in an earlier lifetime and returned as John to serve Jesus. It was all part of a plan. All of the souls that were close to Jesus served him in many previous lifetimes and earned their place to be close to God in heaven. Just as each soul that returns to an incarnate life has a soul family in heaven, there is also a soul family of God. Those souls are selected to return to lead others toward the service of the supreme Deity.

There are members of his soul family that walk the earth today or have recently passed. In this book, we will introduce you to two of them that have recently passed, Mother Teresa and Reverend Billy Graham. They were sent back to spread the word of God and were quite successful. There are chapters devoted to receiving messages from each of them. God is still sending members of his soul family back to spread his words through the miracle of reincarnation. This book is proof that God is still trying to spread his words, bring others to the love of God, and spread that love throughout the world.

Other members of his soul family remain in heaven and act as spirit guides to help direct humans on Earth. Souls like Saint Peter, Saint Paul, Saint Augustine, the Blessed Mother Mary, and others hear your prayers and attempt to influence your lives for good. God works in many ways through his trusted souls in heaven. The challenge is to get humans to understand the messages of love from these ascended souls.

Humans have many opportunities to communicate with members of the soul family of God or the angels that assist them. They can reach them through prayer, meditation, or simply just by speaking to them. The words in this book are proof that God communicates with humans in many ways.

CHAPTER 3

Moses

Just who was Moses? Many remember the name from the famous 1960 movie, where Charlton Heston portrayed him as a religious zealot that saved the Israelites from the cruel Egyptian Pharaoh. Much is written about him in the book of Exodus, but, as with any event taking place over 3,500 years ago, how much of his story actually took place, and how much was made up by those who manipulated the gospels through time? Exodus tells us that Moses was raised by Pharaoh's daughter and led the Israelites to the Promised Land as God carried out miracles like parting the waters of the Red Sea. It is written that he saw God in the form of a burning bush, wandered around in the desert for 40 years, and died at the age of 120 before reaching the Promised Land. In this chapter, we will interview one of the most famous of the holy spirits. The spirit that lived his life as Moses began the session by delivering a wonderful message:

Yes, I am here with you tonight, and I am so happy to be able to once again bring you a message and speak to the people. As you are aware, it has been many years since I had the opportunity to speak the words of God. It was over 3,500 years ago that my spirit walked the earth in the body of Moses, and it has not been since that time that I have had the opportunity to speak in person. So I want to thank Barry and Connie for this opportunity.

I want all of you to know that God watches over each and every one of you, that he is with you, and he is well aware of this mission that he has brought you back for: to help spread his words of love. Each of the holy spirits that have come through has had wonderful messages for you. Each has told you of the growing evil that we face in the world today. Have no doubts that Satan is continually active and is doing his best to defeat your country. When I walked the earth as Moses, I had to fight with the Egyptians; I had to plead with them to allow me to take my people out of their country.

Evil was rampant at those times, and as they worshipped their many gods, they resented the fact that I and my people spoke of the one God. He is a loving God! He is a God for everyone, not only members of the Christian religion but members of other faiths as well. There are members of the Hindu faith, Muslims, and many other world religions that can find their way into his heaven without speaking of him directly. What is important is that each of you lives a life of love and shows that love to others. If you have hatred in your hearts, you are not speaking the words of our Lord. When our Lord walked the earth, he had no hatred in his heart. He only showed love to others. Unfortunately, many discarded his messages, and many continued to worship their pagan images.

Know this! I serve our God on this side of the veil! Know this as well, that he is present on your side of the veil, and just because you cannot see him does not mean you should ever doubt his presence. When I was young, I had times I doubted his presence; he came to me and showed me that not only did he exist, but he had incredible powers when he wished to exert them. This is a time that he is leading the people of Earth to exert their free will, and hopefully they will use that free will to show the love that our Lord showed and to bring others into his way of living. Your government today is attempting in many ways to destroy your country. Your country, the United States, is the pillar of security for the world; without the United States, other countries will fill the gap, and the world will be plunged into the darkness of Satan. Think about your actions; think about whether they will fulfill the wishes of God. If you have any doubts, follow the pathway of love and help for others. Know this as well: our Lord and Savior is very unhappy with the killing of innocents! Abortion is a terrible sin, and as secularism grows, abortion will grow as well. Have no doubts that if you approve of abortion, you are not following the words of God. With that message, I will now begin to answer the questions that I assisted Barry in writing for tonight.

Much is written about Moses throughout the book of Exodus and throughout the Old Testament. I inquired about the accuracy of the writings in the Old Testament.

Some are accurate, and some are not. For instance, I just told you my age when I passed; I did not live to be well into my hundreds. I also did cross over into Judea and actually crossed back to where the Israelites were camping; unfortunately, I was very old at that point and became sick and unable to lead any longer. The writings are accurate about the basic fact that the Israelites went from Egypt to the land that was promised to them. Many of the details are exaggerated, such as the wandering for 40 years. The fact that God did part the waters and killed the army of the Pharaoh is also accurate. He did not part the entire width of the Red Sea for us, but he definitely did part the waters in a major miracle.

There is much about the life of Moses you will find amazing. In this chapter, I will attempt to separate fact from exaggerated fiction.

Israelites, the Family of Abraham

We are told in biblical teachings that the various tribes of Israel migrated to Egypt, where they lived for approximately 400 years and were led to the Promised Land by Moses. We began the question session by asking Moses, "Who were the Israelites?"

The Israelites were the descendants of Abraham. They were taught of the one God. There were times where Israelites strayed from that belief, but they were, in the beginning, the chosen people of God.

I asked, "What made the Israelites special?" He replied:

Abraham created the tribe of Israelites, and they spoke of the one God.

At a time when many Gods were worshipped in many pagan forms, a reverence to the one God would have been unique. The Old Testament book of Exodus is dedicated to the plight of the Israelites. I inquired who wrote the book of Exodus.

The book of Exodus was written at a later time based upon stories that were told among the elders of the Israelites. Some of what was written was grossly exaggerated, but the general theme of the book of Exodus does portray the journey of the Israelites.

"Why did the Israelites settle in Egypt?"

At the time, Egypt was the center of the known world; they provided relative safety and food and a type of government that, even though they were often at odds with the Israelites, it was a composition of governments that was required for their safety.

"Where did they live prior to settling in Egypt?"

They were basically wanderers. They lived in what is now northern Africa, on the edge of what you now refer to as the Mediterranean Sea. They basically hunted and gathered food and migrated to settle in Egypt.

Early Life of Moses

We are told in the Bible that Moses was born to Israelite parents at a time when the Pharaoh feared that their tribe was gathering too much strength and ordered the death of the male children in an attempt to slow the growth of their tribe. There is much uncertainty as to when Moses was born or even if he actually existed. I inquired in what year he was born.

I was born at what you would refer to as to 1,600 years before the birth of our Lord.

"Where were you born?"

I was born in Egypt, in a small town on the Nile River.

"So were you Israelite or Egyptian?"

I was born an Israelite.

"Were you born into the family of Abraham?"

Yes, I was a descendant from the family of Abraham.

"Did you have any brothers or sisters?"

I had one brother and one sister.

The gospels tell a story about the mother of Moses attempting to save his life by putting the baby in a small raft and hiding him among the reeds growing on the edge of the Nile River. One of the daughters of the Pharaoh supposedly discovered the baby and raised it as her own. I asked him if he was adopted by a daughter of Pharaoh. His reply was this:

Yes; at that time, Egyptians were growing fearful of the growth of the Israelites in their country, and they feared that they would oppose some of the teachings of the Pharaoh. The Pharaoh demanded that the male children of the Israelites be massacred. My life was saved when my birth mother built a small raft and tried to hide me on the edge of the Nile River. A servant of the Pharaoh's daughter found me and took me to her. She adopted me and raised me as an Egyptian member of royalty.

Writings in the scriptures indicate that Moses had a very complex personality and possibly a speech disability. I inquired if he had a speech defect.

Yes; when I talked, I stuttered. I had problems communicating with others. When I was young, the Egyptian rulers thought I should be put to death because of my speech defect. The Pharaoh's daughter protected me from that fate.

"How would you describe yourself?"

I was very self-conscious because of my speech defect. I was very nervous around people because it was so difficult for me to communicate. Some would describe me as being aloof or standing alone, but it was because of my insecurities of my speech abilities.

"Who was Aaron?"

Aaron was my brother.

"Did Aaron speak for you?"

Yes; since I had difficulty in speaking to others, I would often have Aaron speak my words to the group of people. I would tell Aaron in my own way what I wanted him to say, and he would speak the words.

I always find it interesting that historic figures that seem bigger than life often had physical problems, like many of us do today.

Time to Leave Egypt

We are told in the book of Exodus that Moses was forced to leave Egypt after killing an Egyptian that was beating an Israelite. I asked him why he had to leave Egypt.

As I grew older and stronger, I began to have differences of opinion with the ruling class in Egypt. There was a time they began to treat the Israelites as their slaves. I attempted to resist cruelty to my people and became involved in an argument that resulted in me injuring one of the Egyptian officials. That was against the law, and I was required to flee for my life.

Score one for the gospel! It is also written that after a period of time, God came to him and commanded that he return to Egypt and lead his people to safety. I inquired what happened to indicate that he would be safe to return to the country where he was raised.

I was very nervous about returning, but I was told through prophecy that I had to return to lead my people to safety. I sent a messenger to the Pharaoh's daughter, and she intervened and allowed for me to return.

"How were you greeted when you returned to Egypt?"

When I returned to Egypt, there were those that wanted to punish me for what I had done in the past; however, the daughter of the Pharaoh protected me from that.

The great prophets had psychic abilities that allowed them to receive messages from the spirit world. I asked Moses to describe his psychic abilities for us.

As a teenager, I began to realize I could communicate with spirits from the other side. I discussed that with the members of my Egyptian family, and they thought that I would be what they would refer to as a seer. I could close my eyes and see figures and hear messages in my head.

"Did you have the ability to heal others?"

Not in the beginning, but as I needed to build confidence in my people to follow me, God gave me the ability to heal others to show that I truly spoke his words.

"How did you convince the people of your psychic abilities?"

Well, I would heal them, for one thing, but I was given the ability to forecast some future events. When those events would happen, the people became convinced that I truly could speak to the other side.

"Did you perform any miracles?"

Yes, I performed multiple miracles, but most of them were healing others. There were times that I would pass on the words of God, as you are doing tonight, and that would be considered a miracle.

I consider what we do a miracle as well!

Conversations with God

Moses is famous for his conversations with God. I asked if God really did appear to him.

> *Yes; not in physical form, but he would appear to me as an angel or perhaps in another form. God has no physical form.*

"Was anyone with you when you saw God?"

> *No; God would come to me when I was alone. He would send me signs; for instance, an angel would appear. I would see an actual angel, and I would know that the angel was speaking the words of God.*

"Why did God appear to you?"

> *Because he needed to give me instructions on how to lead my people.*

One of the most famous parts of the book of Exodus is when God appeared to Moses in the form of a burning bush. I inquired if there really was a burning bush.

> *No, there was never a burning bush. My messages would come to me in the form of angels speaking to me.*

"What was God's message?"

> *His message was that I should lead the Israelites out of Egypt.*

God felt very strongly that it was time to end the oppression of the Israelites in Egypt, and he assigned that task to Moses.

Let My People Go!

The Old Testament tells us that when Moses arrived back in Egypt, the Pharaoh was emphatic about not letting the Israelites leave Egypt. I asked him why the Pharaoh would not allow the Israelites to leave. He replied:

When I spoke to the Pharaoh, I asked if I would be allowed to lead them out of Egypt, to their own land. The Egyptians were becoming more and more accustomed to using Israelites as slaves, and they did not want to lose that source of workers.

That decision on the part of the Egyptian ruler would prove to be a huge mistake. My next question inquired what happened when the Pharaoh refused to allow the Israelites to leave.

I received a message from God that he would intervene and act in such a manner as to make the Egyptians allow the Israelites to leave Egypt. The angel told me that Egypt would come under many problems.

I think "many problems" is a bit of an understatement. We are told that as a result of not being given permission to leave, Egypt endured many plagues. I inquired if the plagues took place.

Yes; there was a time that many things happened in the country of Egypt. There was indeed a time that the country was placed in darkness, and because of that darkness, crop failures happened, and many bugs and other rodents and insects spread sickness and in general caused huge amounts of pain to the Egyptian people.

I had viewed a documentary that attempted to correlate the plagues of Egypt with a huge volcanic eruption that took place on the island of Santorini in Greece around 1600 BC. The show concluded that the sky was darkened by the volcanic ash, and the plagues followed the darkening of the skies. I asked Moses if the sky darkened because of a volcanic eruption. His answer confirmed the theory.

At the time we were going through the darkening of the sky, I believed it was solely because of the action of God. After I arrived over here, I learned that God uses natural occurrences for his own purposes. The sky was darkened by a volcanic eruption of what you now call the country of Greece. The cloud from the volcano is what caused the darkness that created the beginnings of what were referred to as plagues.

We had been told before that God used natural events to carry out his will. Next, I inquired why the Pharaoh changed his mind and allowed the Israelites to leave Egypt.

The plagues that were overcoming the Egyptian people seemed to be growing worse and worse. I kept telling him that it was occurring because he was not allowing the Israelites to leave. His seers and top officials finally recommended that he allow the Israelites to leave as a test to see if things would truly improve.

The Exodus

When the Pharaoh decided to let the Israelites go, one of the most famous journeys in history began. Led by Moses, the Israelite people began a journey across some of the harshest terrain of the ancient world. We are told in the gospels that God provided food for the group by supplying manna. I asked Moses what the manna was that was provided by God. His answer made a lot of sense:

As we would go through the desert, we would be led to different oases or places where water was available, and in those places, we would find plants that we could eat and animals that we could butcher to sustain ourselves.

Shortly after the journey began, the Pharaoh changed his mind and sent his army in pursuit of the Israelites. I asked if Moses knew that he was being pursued by the Egyptian army.

Yes; after a period of time, the angel came to me and warned me that we were being pursued. He also told us not to worry, that God would protect us.

It must have been quite upsetting to find out that the most powerful army of the ancient world was in hot pursuit. God was about to perform one of his most amazing miracles to assure the safety of his people. In previous sessions, I had asked if Moses parted the Red Sea. Jesus had replied:

God parted the sea.

Hard to argue with that answer! The documentary I watched had an interesting theory. The physical features of Egypt have changed in the 3,600 years since the Exodus, and apparently there was a very large lake and marsh called the Reeded Sea that existed on what would have been the path to Judea. It proposed a theory that God actually parted the Reeded Sea and the ancient writings mistakenly referred to the Red Sea. I asked Moses if it was the Red Sea that was parted by God.

God parted a large waterway for us, but it was not actually what you now refer to as the Red Sea; there was a large lake and marsh area that God separated and allowed us to escape.

"How long did it take for the Israelites to cross the parted sea?"

It took about two days. At the end of the second day, the Pharaoh's army was approaching, and God determined that he would end the threat to the Israelites once and for all, and the waters of the great lake returned, and the army of the Egyptians was destroyed.

The book of Numbers states that God became unhappy with the Israelites because they turned their back on God, and so he forced them to wander in the desert for 40 years. I asked Moses if they were forced to wander for 40 years in the desert.

No, that is not true. It took us quite a while to get through some of the drier portions, but we did not wander for 40 years in the desert.

"Were you with them at all times?"

I was always with the people; I would try to lead them, and when we felt we were headed in the wrong direction or that we were lost, the angel of God would come to us, and he would give direction. They provided sustenance for us and showed us where I should lead the people.

"How long was the total journey of the Israelites?"

In your time, I would guess that it took us three or four years to complete the journey.

That time frame certainly makes a lot more sense.

The gospel of Numbers tells us that Moses and the Israelites fought with the Midianites, a tribe that lived in the Sinai at the time of the Exodus. In that gospel, it is stated that the Midianites were not only defeated but that the women and children were massacred. I asked Moses if the Israelites massacred the Midianites. His response was this:

We did engage in battle with the Midianites, but we did show mercy to those that survived. God would never have us murder the innocent women and children.

His answer made a lot more sense than what is in the Bible.

"Who was Joshua?"

Joshua was the person that God selected to take over for me when I reached the age where I could no longer efficiently lead my people.

"Where did you die?"

I died very close to what is now Judea.

"Did you die on Mount Nebo?"

I died near Mount Nebo.

"Where are you buried?"

I am buried at the base of what you now refer to as Mount Nebo.

"How old were you when you died?"

In your years, I was around 78 years old.

So much for him living into his 120s.

God's Commandments

All of Christianity reveres the Ten Commandments given to Moses by God. I asked Moses to describe how he received the commandments from God.

Moses and the Ten Commandments – Rembrandt – 1659 – Gemaldegalerie, Berlin

Yes; the angel told me that I would be receiving a special message from God. I needed to get away from the rest of the people so that I could focus on the messages I would be receiving. I climbed what you now refer to as Mount Sinai and found a secluded place. The angel of God came to me and in my mind gave me multiple commands for the people to live by. I took those commands and inscribed them on stone, because at the time, I didn't have any other type of material, so I scraped them on stone, and we tried to preserve them.

Not quite as exciting as the biblical version, but this explanation seems to be a bit more believable. Next, I asked how many commandments he received.

> *I basically received six or seven. Foremost was, I was told that individuals should not take innocent lives. I was given a commandment that marriage should be honored. I was given other simple commands; mainly they were focused around the love of God.*

It has been thought that Moses was the author of the books of Genesis, Exodus, and Numbers. My next question was this: "Did you personally ever write any gospels?"

> *No; there were those among us that tried to make some notes, but I never personally was involved writing any of the gospels.*

Modern scholars believe that the books of Genesis and Exodus were not written until around 600 BC, around 1,000 years after the Exodus. It is not hard to imagine how the stories were changed over such a long period of time.

Soul Life after Moses

Since his passing 3,500 years ago, Moses has gone home to heaven, where he has been serving God. I inquired if he had ever reincarnated since his life as Moses.

> *No; I have chosen to serve our Lord and God from this side of the veil. Should he ask me to return, I most certainly would return and do his bidding, but I have not walked on the earth since I walked in the body of Moses.*

"Did you serve God on Earth in any lifetime before you walked the earth as Moses?"

> *Yes; I had served Abraham at an earlier time. I tried to help him to teach his people of the one God, but nothing is written of me in that lifetime.*

"What is your current role in heaven?"

I do what my God wishes me to do. He instructed me to come to you tonight and speak to the people in your group. He wants me to actively be involved in trying to stop the spread of Satan in your current world.

Connie asked, "Do Barry and I know you when we are on the other side?"

Yes; when you were on the other side, you were one with us. That is why you and Connie were chosen to return to carry our words to the multitudes.

Connie and I still find it hard to believe we rub elbows with the likes of Moses while on the other side. Since he basically saved the Israelite tribes that would eventually form the Jewish nation, I asked him his opinion of the current Jewish nation.

The current Jewish nation in some ways has lost its bearings from what God intended. For instance, they do not accept that Jesus was the Messiah; that is a major mistake for them, and it is not until they return home that they understand the error of their judgment.

Our time spent with this true man of God has been amazing, and the information given to us makes the story of the Exodus more believable.

A Final Message

We asked the spirit of Moses if he had a final message for us.

Yes; tonight was an honor to speak to all of you. I have enjoyed once again to have others listen to my words. I will return again if I am requested, because it is very important that Satan is defeated! It is very important that others are brought to know and love God! It is important that others know that Jesus was God incarnate and that he speaks the words that he was sent back to speak. He lived among humans. He suffered. He loved, and he died at the hands of humans. That is what free will did to our Lord. It is vitally imperative that you do not allow free will to destroy humans on Earth. You are now reaching a point in time when you can assure mutual destruction of all. It is time to put away your weapons of mass destruction and spread love for one another. The advanced cultures in your galaxy learned this lesson many, many years ago. There is nothing to be gained through mutual destruction. Humans will not be destroyed by God; humans can only be destroyed by their own actions. Take to heart what I am speaking tonight. Know that God is with you but that he will allow your free will and ego to determine your evolution. Speak of God at all times. Never fear that you will be ignored, and never think that you are alone. Even through dark times, he is with you; when you are in pain, he is with you. The energy of God shares your suffering and your burdens. Pray to him, and your prayers will be answered. If you believe in God, have no fear, because you will join him in the realms of heaven. With those words, I am going to leave you tonight. Thank you for listening; I enjoyed speaking, and bless you and may God be with you! Amen.

Since this interview, the spirit of Moses has returned to us on several occasions, contributing on radio shows and supplying us with additional information. His spirit continues to be a true servant of God.

CHAPTER 4

John the Baptist

John the Baptist is one of the most interesting individuals mentioned in the Bible. Not only is he the individual that baptized Jesus so he could begin his ministries, but he was Elijah reincarnated. Elijah was a prophet that was sent to Earth hundreds of years before the birth of Christ. He spoke of the one God, performed miracles, and predicted the coming of the Messiah. His reincarnation is referred to multiple times in the gospels, especially in the book of Matthew.

Message of John the Baptist

We were blessed by his spirit presence during one of our Facebook Live sessions, and he began by giving us the following message:

I am here tonight because Jesus requested that I come and tell you the story of my love of the one God. I was chosen to baptize our Lord because of my service in past lives. We had lived many lifetimes together, and I was very trusted to carry out his messages. I had lived 470 years earlier as Elijah; in that lifetime, I spoke of the coming of the Messiah. In that lifetime, there were many people that worshipped many gods. My role in that lifetime was to tell them of the one God. It was very difficult, but I managed to convince many. It was not until my lifetime with Jesus that the prophecy of the coming of the Messiah was fulfilled. Jesus was God and the Messiah! He came to us in that lifetime to tell all what was required to advance in the realms of heaven. Many listened and followed his words; his words were in many ways historical. His simple teachings of love and kindness were complicated by the churches to strengthen the powers of man. We were very disappointed over here by what was happening but decided to let free will take its course. As you can now all tell, free will is strengthening the power of Satan. Now is the time when you must all make a stand for God. If you fail in bringing back his words, the future of mankind is in doubt.

We are here tonight to strengthen your resolve to lead others to God. Barry and Connie walked the earth with us, as did many of you. You have been brought together in this time of need to renew faith in our God; that is his very simple command. He will bless those that follow his commands, and they will find peace in his holy heaven. Learn, and lead those who will listen! Those that do not listen will not enjoy all the benefits of his heaven. I will now answer some questions, and at the end Jesus will bless all of you.

Life as Elijah

The soul of John the Baptist is quite unique in that the Bible actually indicates he was Elijah reincarnated. I began our channeling session with him by asking if he had lived many lifetimes on Earth before his soul was selected to live the lifetime of Elijah. He replied:

No; that was my first life on Earth, but I had lived many, many lifetimes in other worlds.

Once again, we see that the holiest of souls have lived many lifetimes and served the one God many times before humans walked the earth. I explored this subject in detail in a chapter entitled "Universal Reincarnation" in my previous book, *Spirits Speak of the Universe*, so I will not go into detail here. My next question addressed how many years Elijah lived before Christ was born.

Four hundred seventy.

"When you were Elijah, how did you know it was your mission to speak of the one God?"

The angels came to me and told me my mission.

"When you were Elijah, what was the main message you spoke?"

I told the people that there was only a single God, and if they continued to worship other gods, they would pay a price in their afterlife.

Elijah lived at the time of the height of the Classical Greek civilization, with all their pagan beliefs. It was also when Alexander the Great was defeating the Persian Empire and spreading Greek power throughout the world. It would have taken a lot of bravery to preach of the one God at such a time of pagan worship, let alone talk about the coming of a Messiah. It would have been very difficult to convince the people of that time that what they had been taught about their gods and the afterlife was not correct. Jesus performed miracles to convince the people, so I asked John if, when he was Elijah, he had the ability to perform miracles. His answer was this:

Yes; that was the only way I could convince others, just as you will have the ability to heal others using the energy of God.

"What was the most important miracle performed by Elijah?"

I rose several people from the dead.

That must have gotten the attention of the people, just as it did when Jesus performed the same miracles.

The gospels state that Elijah made a grand entry into heaven. Second Kings 2:11–12 states the following:

As they were walking along and talking together, suddenly a chariot of fire and horses of fire appeared and separated the two of them, and Elijah went up to heaven in a whirlwind. Elisha saw this and cried out, "My father! My father! The chariots and horsemen of Israel!" And Elisha saw him no more. Then he took hold of his garment and tore it in two. (New International Version)

I asked John if he was taken to heaven in a chariot.

No; my soul went to heaven like every other soul. That story was made up by man.

Tradition holds that he never died but was taken to heaven, to return on Judgment Day. Since he alluded to the fact that his soul went to heaven like every soul, it appears that he really did die like any other human. I asked how old Elijah was when he passed.

Ninety years old.

Once again, we see that the early writers of the gospels made up a story to make the death of Elijah more memorable. I asked if, when he lived his life as John, he knew that he was Elijah reincarnated. He replied:

No; I only learned that when I returned home.

There is no doubt that the true home of a soul is heaven.

Along Comes John the Baptist

I inquired if he wanted to tell us anything else about Elijah before we moved on to discuss his life as John the Baptist.

No; my life as John is of greater importance.

In my research, I ran across a statement that John was related to Jesus. To that question, he answered:

No, we were not related.

"Who were your parents?"

My mother's name was Ruth.

"What was your father's name?"

His name was Matthew.

"How old was your mother when you were born?"

She was 21.

"How old was your father when you were born?"

He was 23.

"How did your father die?"

He passed of natural causes.

"In what country were you born?"

I was born in Judea.

It appears that John lived a normal life as a child.

A Special Message

By the time John met Jesus, he had learned of his mission to preach of the one God and the coming of the Messiah. I inquired how he learned that his mission in life as John was to inform the people that the Messiah was about to appear. He answered:

I was told by angels. They informed me my life was very special and that I would play a major role in the life of the Messiah.

The angels and spirit guides have a way of informing individuals about their life paths. One event that happened during the lifetime of John was King Herod the

Great ordering the massacre of the innocents in an attempt to kill the baby Jesus. I asked John if he was affected by King Herod's actions.

I learned of it later and was saddened by Herod's cruelty

By the time he met Jesus, John had been preaching to the people and had a following of his own. I inquired as to the content of his teachings before he met Jesus.

I spoke of the one God.

I asked how he learned that his role in life was to preach of the one God.

Once again, it was told to me by angels.

"When you were John, did you ever perform any miracles?"

No, those were only performed by our Lord.

"How did you meet Jesus?"

We were introduced by a friend.

"When you first saw Jesus, did you know he was the Messiah?"

No; the angels came to me and told me that I had met God.

That is certainly not a message that you hear every day. "How long did you know Jesus before you were informed by the angels that you had met the Messiah?"

Several months.

John was part of a well-conceived plan to introduce Jesus to the fulfillment of his life plan.

Why Baptism?

I was never really sure of the real purpose of baptism. *Merriam-Webster* defines baptism as

> **1a:** *a Christian sacrament marked by ritual use of water and admitting the recipient to the Christian community*
> **b:** *a non-Christian rite using water for ritual purification*
> **c:** *Christian Science : purification by or submergence in Spirit*
> **2:** *an act, experience, or ordeal by which one is purified, sanctified, initiated, or named.*

I asked John the significance of the act of baptism. He replied:

> *Baptism is symbolic of the rebirth of your soul in the service of God.*

"Were you ever baptized?"

> *No; there was no one to baptize me.*

I guess it would have been very difficult to find anyone, since he was the first to baptize others. I inquired how he learned about baptism.

> *I was also shown this by the angels.*

"Is there one angel in particular that gave you more messages than others?"

> *Yes; Gabriel was my main angel.*

Gabriel must have been very busy during this time frame. He was also the angel that told Mary she was with child. "Do you still see Gabriel?"

> *Yes; he still plays a very important role.*

I always wondered why God, reincarnated in the form of Jesus, needed the act of baptism for him to begin his ministries. When I asked John, the answer was this:

The act released the powers of God. Until that time, the powers of God were dormant within him.

We had been told before that Jesus did not perform any miracles before he began his ministries, and my previous book stressed the normality of the first 28 years of his life. My next question asked what words John spoke at the baptism of Jesus.

My words were, "God, please bless and keep your Son and let him now go forward in your name."

His words were very simple and obviously very effective. "How old were you when you baptized Jesus?"

Thirty-two.

That means he was approximately four years older than Jesus at the time of his baptism. I inquired if he also baptized the wife and children of Jesus.

Yes; they also received my blessings.

"Did you ever baptize Mary and Joseph?"

No; they were raised in the Jewish faith but spoke only of the one God.

"Did you know the wife and children of Jesus?"

Yes; we were very friendly, and I spent much time in their home.

We were told before that John and the family of Jesus were very friendly. "Did you ever join Jesus in his ministries?"

Only in the very beginning. His path was separate from mine.

The life plans of John and Jesus were well planned before they returned as humans, and the angels guided them on that path. The Bible states that John lived a very strange lifestyle, wearing camel's hair and living in caves. When I asked him if that was true, he answered:

I lived a normal life. There were times I had to live in a cave, and I did wear camel's hair to keep warm.

I guess you cannot blame a man for trying to keep warm. After John left Jesus, he preached the word of the one God and the presence of the Messiah. His words would get him in big trouble with Herod Antipas, the ruler of Galilee and son of King Herod the Great.

Head on a Platter

A little background is required to understand why John was martyred. Herod Antipas, the ruler of Galilee under the Roman Empire, divorced his wife Phasaelis to marry Herodias, the wife of his brother, Herod Philip. John preached that this union was incest and against the will of God. His words enraged Herodias, and she forced Herod to have John imprisoned. Herodias had a daughter named Salome. It is written that Herod did not want to kill John, fearing a Jewish uprising, and asked him to leave the area ruled by Herod Antipas. John refused to leave and chose to remain in jail.

Herod Antipas was planning to have a huge birthday celebration and wanted Salome to dance for the guests. He offered to grant her one wish in return for her dancing. When she asked her mother for advice on what to ask for, she told her to ask for John's head on a platter. Herod complied with her request, and

Beheading of John the Baptist – Caravaggio – 1607 – St. John's Cathedral, Valetta, Italy

John was executed. Herod Antipas gained notoriety forever, and Salome's dance became famous. I hope the dance was worth the price the king would pay when he got to heaven. I thought I would investigate what really happened, so I asked John why he was arrested by Herod Antipas. He answered:

He did not like what I preached about his incestuous marriage. His marriage was against the teachings of God. He was very upset by my words.

I think "upset" was an understatement! I asked John what role Salome played in his death.

She made Antipas cut off my head because her mother was the object of my teachings.

In this instance, it appears that the details written in the gospels concerning the death of John the Baptist are correct. One thing is certain: the early teachers of the words of God had little fear of death and were true to their convictions.

Home in Heaven

The soul energy that was the incarnate forms of Elijah and John the Baptist was entrusted with a very important role in the life of Jesus. For this soul to be entrusted with such a responsibility, it must be highly ascended and literally be at the right hand of God. I asked some questions about his role in heaven, starting with what role he currently played.

I try to guide others who are following our God. It has become very difficult. That is why you and Connie were sent back.

That last statement caught me by surprise. I asked if he knew Connie and me when we were in heaven. He replied:

Yes, you walk with us in the service of God.

I have mentioned many times that we all enter a life with a well-defined plan. I asked, "Did you help with Connie's and my life plan?"

Of course.

Those statements were a bit overwhelming. I asked if he had reincarnated since the time of Christ.

Not on your planet, but I have been on others.

Once again, the holy spirit was reaffirming the galactic power of God and the role played by the holy soul family throughout the galaxy. It appears that Connie and I play a role in spreading the words of God by being his messengers as well.

Much is written about the remains of the saints. It is said that the remains of John the Baptist are buried in Sebastia, at St. John the Baptist Mosque. I asked if that was correct.

Yes, my physical remains are there, but my soul is with our Lord here in heaven.

Since he referred to Connie and me, I asked if he had a personal message for us.

Yes; walk with your head held high, knowing that God is with you and watches over you. God knows that you are trying your best. In the future, all will know that you and Connie have an undying love of God in your hearts.

There is not much you can say after receiving such messages from one of the holiest of spirits. As we have walked this path, Connie and I have come to realize the responsibility that has been placed upon us: that of bringing you, the people, the true messages of Jesus and his apostles. We have gathered a group of followers, so I asked John if he had a final message for the members of our group. He replied:

> *Heed my words that were spoken earlier, and know the importance of your mission.*

A Message From Jesus

At this time of rapidly spreading atheism and evil, his words are indeed very important. In his message, he mentioned that Jesus would come through with a message for all. Here is the message of Jesus that ended our session on that night:

> *I am also here to tell all of my love and kindness for all. My words must leave an impression and bring others to my preachings, or human evolution is in danger. God bless all of you listening. Follow my words, and you will be with me in my realm. Amen!*

We have learned that John the Baptist is an amazing soul and sits at the right hand of God in heaven, a place earned by serving God many times during many lifetimes. His appearance was a blessing to us all, and his message an inspiration to all of us.

CHAPTER 5

Saint Andrew

The Bible actually tells us very little about Saint Andrew. It states that he was the first apostle, the brother of Peter, and a member of the inner circle of the disciples of Jesus. There are two different versions of how Andrew met Jesus. Matthew 4:18–20 tells us the following:

> *And Jesus walking by the Sea of Galilee, saw two brethren, Simon who is called Peter and Andrew his brother, casting a net into the sea. And he saith to them: Come ye after me, and I will make you to be fishers of men and they immediately leaving their nets, followed him. King James Version*

Saint Andrew – Masaccio – 1426 – J. Paul Getty Museum, Pittsburg, PA.

The book of John tells us that Andrew was a follower of John the Baptist. The book of John 1:40–42 tells us the following:

> *One of the two who had heard what John said, and followed him, was Andrew, the brother of Simon Peter. He, first of all, found his own brother Simon, and told him, We have discovered the Messiah (which means, the Christ), and brought him to Jesus. New Living Version*

There is no real proof of how Andrew died. A popular myth states that he was crucified on an X-shaped cross, and the Cross of Saint Andrew is an important symbol today. As you will learn, much of what we have been told about Saint Andrew will be refuted in our interview, conducted in October of 2018. Here is his message from that interview:

I am here tonight to bring you the words of our Lord. I was honored to walk the earth with him and to serve him. To know our Lord was to know the purest of love and kindness. I never heard him utter a word in anger; all he did was show kindness and love to all that were around him. I watched him perform miracles; they were incredible to see. I knew him as few others knew him. I was honored to be trusted and to be among his inner circle. I, as well as the others, was heartbroken when his life was taken by the Romans. I tried to carry on his works as best I could. I traveled to many countries, speaking the words that he spoke. Many listened, but many did not, just as you are having problems finding people to believe that you are really receiving true messages from us. We also had much opposition to what we were saying. The Romans, in particular, did not want to hear about there being a single God. They worshipped many and believed that teaching the one God undermined the power of the Roman Empire.

You will find as you progress that more and more people will pay attention to what you are saying. When Barry's next book comes out, many will begin to pay attention and listen. What is in that book was given to him by our Lord and many of the holy saints. Know that what is in that book speaks the truth and the reality of what was spoken by our Lord. Tonight, I am very appreciative to be able to once again speak the words of love that were spoken by Jesus the Christ. He was the Messiah that was sent to Earth; know that his words are the words of God. They are one and the same. Love of one another is the most important teaching that I will speak of tonight. Know as well that Satan is growing in strength, especially in the killing of innocent children in the womb. Taking a life is an unforgivable sin. Those that allow it can find redemption by realizing the error of what they've done, but for those performing the acts, there will be no redemption. Tonight, once again, is very special; as I have been asked to speak with you, others will follow. Study what is spoken during these sessions; they reflect the true teachings of God. I will now answer some questions.

Once again, we were honored with a very inspiring message from a servant of God.

Soul History of Andrew

We have discussed the soul family of God in previous interviews. I asked Andrew to tell us about the soul family of God.

There are those souls that have advanced through thousands of lifetimes in service to our God. Those souls are elevated to the highest level of heaven, and they are called upon to return and serve our God. You and Connie have been sent back as members of that family to bring people his words.

"Did you ever serve our Lord on this planet before you walked the earth as Andrew?"

I only lived one human life, and that was as Andrew.

"Did you serve our Lord on other planets?"

Yes; that is what we have done for thousands of lifetimes in the past. Remember that the human race is very young and has much to learn.

I think the part about the human race having a lot to learn is a bit of an understatement. I asked if he would describe his service on the other planets.

It is very difficult to describe those services, because humans are incapable of understanding what takes place on those other planets. There are emotions that have never been felt by humans; there are languages that humans will never comprehend. In time, hopefully, humans will advance so they can understand those things.

Having written two books on channeled information about extraterrestrials, this was an answer I had heard multiple times. The complexities of the physical and emotional structures on other planets must be staggering to understand. My alien spirit friend, Mou, had told me on many occasions that the answer to a question was beyond my ability to comprehend.

Personal History of Andrew

I started to delve into his personal history by asking in what year he was born.

I was born approximately four years after the birth of our Lord.

Keep in mind that the individuals living in the time of Christ did not have access to calendars. It is not uncommon to have discrepancies in time references.

"Were you the brother of Peter?"

Yes; Peter was my older brother.

My next question addressed where he was born.

I was born on the shores of Galilee. My family lived in a small town.

Since his childhood took place before the birth of Christianity, I inquired as to the religion he was introduced to as a child.

I was raised in the Roman tradition of paganism.

"How were you introduced to Jesus?"

I was working, and our Lord approached me with several of his friends.

"What was your occupation?"

I was a tax collector for the Romans.

Interesting answer. The Bible refers to Andrew and his brother as fishermen. I asked if he could read or write.

Yes; my family educated me, and I could both read and write. It was a requirement to be a tax collector for the Romans.

It would have been very unusual for a fisherman to be able to read and write. There were not any public schools in those days. So much for the story about him being a "fisher of men." It is also written that he was a disciple of John the Baptist. I inquired if that was correct.

I knew who John was, but I was not a disciple; I had heard that he spoke of the one God.

"Were you one of the first to join Jesus?"

Yes, I was among the first. He came to me and asked me to follow him in spreading word of the one God. I had heard of him and recognized who he was.

"At what age did you meet Jesus?"

I was 22 years old.

I am amazed at how young these individuals were whose words would help change the world. "Were you married when you decided to follow Jesus?

No; I was considering marriage, but when I met our Lord, I realized that I would be consumed by following him and would have no time for marriage.

It was not an easy life, following Jesus as he spoke the message of the one God.

Life with Jesus

I can only imagine what it would have been like to have known Jesus in life. In Andrew's earlier message, he spoke briefly of what it was like to walk with our Lord. I asked if he would elaborate on what it was like to be with him.

It was most amazing to be with him. I never saw another person with such love in his heart. You could feel his loving energy when you were near him; his eyes showed a powerful energy. When you held his hand, you knew you were close to God.

Andrew was very close to our Lord and traveled with him to many events. I asked if he had ever observed Jesus performing miracles. He replied:

I was blessed to have observed many miracles performed by our Lord.

"Were you with Jesus when he fed the fish to the multitudes?"

Yes, I was present, but the writing in the Bible was greatly exaggerated. He did feed many, but not near the number suggested in the gospels.

"Can you tell us about the Multiplication of the Loaves miracle?"

Yes; I was again with him, but the story in the gospel is much exaggerated. He did feed many persons, but probably not more than 100.

Once again, we hear that many of the events in the New Testament have been grossly exaggerated through the years. I inquired as to his role among the disciples. Andrew answered:

I assisted in keeping track of the funds that paid for our travels. I also would take some notes when he spoke, but mainly I used my education to serve our Lord.

This was clearly not the role of an uneducated fisherman.

One of the most important moments in the life of Jesus occurred when he met with his followers and disciples on the Mount of Olives before he was arrested by the Romans. I asked Andrew about the details of the Last Supper.

There were around 45 or 50 of us present on the Mount of Olives on that last evening. He told us that he would be leaving us. Many of us were in tears of sadness.

We could not comprehend life without having him to lead us. He told us that he expected us to carry on his messages, that they were very important, and that his words would be remembered forever.

It is written that Andrew feared that the earth would end with the passing of our Lord. I inquired if he asked Jesus about any signs of the end of the earth.

Yes; I worried that life on Earth would end without our Lord. He told me that life would continue without him but that man would have to follow his teachings if humans were to exist.

As you are aware, Andrew and most of the disciples were in hiding during the Crucifixion of Jesus because they feared for their own lives. I asked how he learned the details of the killing of Christ.

We were not present at the Crucifixion. Sadly, we feared for our own lives. The two Marys were present, and they described to us what happened.

"Did you see Jesus after the Resurrection?"

Yes; he appeared to us on two different occasions. When we saw him, he still bore the marks of the nails on the cross and the spear mark in his chest. When he appeared, we all cried like babies, thinking that he would be remaining with us. Unfortunately, he came to assure us that he was born again and that we would join him in heaven.

Life after the Death of Jesus

After the death of Jesus, Andrew preached the words of Jesus. There are many rumors about where he preached and how he met his demise. He is the patron saint of Scotland, Georgia, Russia, Ukraine, Barbados, Greece, and many other countries. When I asked him where he preached after the death of Jesus, he replied:

I began teaching in Judea, but I realized others were spreading his words locally as well. I decided to try to spread the word in countries that were not being served.

I eventually went to Africa, because I was not aware of anyone else going to that country.

"Did you ever preach in what is now Russia?"

No; I did venture into Persia but never went as far as Russia.

"Were you ever in Scotland?"

No; once again, I did not venture that far.

As we see from his replies, the stories of his travels were also exaggerated. I could not find any information concerning the message that was taught by Andrew. I asked if he would clarify his message to the people.

I taught a very simple message. I taught that love for God and for others is the most critical lesson to be learned. I taught that if you loved God and led a good life, you would join the Lord in heaven. Our message was very simple. It had to be so that it was understood by the multitudes that had little or no education.

"Did you ever speak of reincarnation?"

Our Lord spoke to us of reincarnation, but it was too difficult a concept to speak to the masses. We simply told them that when they passed, they would join our Lord in heaven.

That is what we have been told by the other holy spirits. We also learned that many of the apostles were given the gift of healing as proof they spoke the words of God. When I inquired if he ever performed any miracles, the answer was this:

Yes; I had the ability to heal others, and I used that ability to prove that I was truly speaking the words of God, just as you will have that ability as well.

Then, as now, it took proof that the individuals were speaking the words of God, and that proof was their ability to heal others.

Crucifixion of Andrew – Peter Paul Rubens - cc 1639 – Fundacion Carlos de Amberes, Madrid, Spain.

Death of Andrew

There is a lot of guesswork involved with the death of Andrew the Apostle, but little is known of his demise. Scholars believe that he was martyred at the city of Patras in Greece. Portions of the cross on which he was said to have been killed are kept in the Church of Saint Andrew at Patras. Portions of his skeleton are also said to be entombed in a special shrine. I started by asking in what country he was killed.

I was killed in what is now Ethiopia.

That was not the answer I was expecting! "Who had you killed?"

The Romans had me executed, because they feared my words would undermine their power. They also did not want me to speak against their pagan gods.

It is amazing how many followed Jesus knowing they would probably be rewarded with a painful death. Their rewards would have to be in heaven. I inquired how he was killed.

I was crucified.

It is said that Andrew requested to be killed on an X-shaped cross because he was not worthy of being crucified in the same manner as our Lord. The Cross of Saint

Andrew is a very important Christian symbol. When I asked if the Romans used an X-shaped cross, the answer was this:

No, I was tied to a regular cross.

"Do any remains of that cross exist today?"

No; at the time, there would have been no reason to save the cross. Keep in mind that the Romans were crucifying many and would have probably used the same cross on others.

That answer certainly makes a lot of sense. I asked his age when he was martyred.

Fifty-four.

"Where are your remains today?"

My remains are scattered, but some are in Italy.

Pope Paul VI in 1964 ordered the remains of Andrew to be given to the Greek Orthodox Church. From that answer, it seems like the Vatican may have not sent the proper remains.

Life after Physical Death

Upon his physical death, he returned to his home in heaven. When I asked him to describe heaven for us, his answer was this:

Heaven is indescribable. The colors are magnificent and vivid. There is no pain. There is no suffering, and there is no grief. While we do watch over family members or friends back on Earth and feel emotions for them, it is not the same. You can travel wherever you want by thinking of the location. There is no food, there is no requirement to sleep; it is beyond anyone's imagination.

Each time I have a spirit describe heaven, it seems like a great place to spend an eternity. "What is your current role in heaven?"

I try to serve our Lord by influencing how humans respond to others. Sometimes it is very frustrating for us, because our commands are being ignored. It is also very hard for us to get our messages through to humans. That is why your work is so important! You have been given the gift to communicate with us and speak our words.

"Have you ever reincarnated since your life as Andrew?"

No; I have served my Lord on this side.

"Are you planning to reincarnate?"

That is totally up to our Lord. If he wants me to return, I would surely follow his orders.

Opinions of Andrew the Apostle

Just because souls are on the other side does not mean that they do not have strong opinions on what is happening back on Earth. We have been getting a lot of criticism about our use of a channeling board to communicate with the other side. I asked Andrew for his opinion of the method we chose to communicate with the spirits. His answer was this:

Your method of communication has been given to you by our Lord. There is no inherent evil in what you do. Anyone that teaches that what you do is evil is not speaking his words. It is very difficult for us to get our messages to humans; the board provides one means of doing that. It is a relatively easy way for us to communicate. We want others to learn the technique so that we can communicate to others when you and Connie are no longer able to do this.

Andrew is a highly revered individual in the Roman Catholic Church. I asked his opinion of the current Roman Catholic Church.

Sadly, we are not pleased with what has happened in the Catholic Church. My name is on many facilities, and I am even patron saint of several countries. Unfortunately, they have let evil enter the church. What they have done to the young is unforgivable. I cry at times when I watch what is taking place. It is our hope that in the future they will return to the true teachings of the love of God.

"What church do you feel most closely reflects the teachings of Jesus?"

There is no church that totally reflects his teachings. Many have wandered far from his words. When there is a church that teaches love, humility, and faith in our Lord, that will be the church that comes closest to his teachings.

"We see much hatred from others concerning our messages; this is especially evident in our messages about homosexuality. Will you comment on this hatred?"

Yes; although homosexuality is not the ordinary way of things, your future in heaven is determined by how you live your life, by how you love God, and what you do with others. Your physical traits can be forgiven if you live the life that is taught by our Lord.

Never underestimate the love of God for all! As we were approaching the end of our interview, I asked Andrew if he had any advice to help the members of the Words of God Then and Now group to help spread the words of God. His answer was this:

Yes; study the transcripts that are available and watch the videos. Understand what is being taught! The better you understand our messages, the better the opportunity you will have to effectively spread the words of God.

Many of the transcripts of the actual sessions are available on my website, http://www.wordsofgodthenandnow.com, and videos of the sessions are on my YouTube channel under my name, Barry Strohm. When I asked Saint Andrew if he had any final message for our listeners, he replied:

> *Yes; I thank God that I have been able to come through to you tonight. I hope that some of my words will inspire and help you to effectively preach the words of God. Many of you have been sent back specifically to advance our teachings and to show others the truth of what our Lord really taught in life. Much has been changed from his original teachings. It is important that humans understand exactly how simple it is to love one another and live a good life. If you truly have the love of God in your hearts, you will join us in heaven. If you teach hatred and fear of our Lord and God, you will find that heaven is not as wonderful as I described. Life in the lower levels is not anything compared to life in the upper levels; that is why souls strive to return, learn, and advance. Tonight, I want you to know that God blesses each and every one of you. And that God is with each and every one of you in your hearts and hopefully in your minds. God bless you all, and good night! Amen!*

It was another very inspiring session with a soul very close to God.

CHAPTER 6

Mary Magdalene, a Female Disciple

Everyone knows the name of Mary Magdalene, but the real facts about her life remain much of a mystery. If you watched *The Da Vinci Code*, your mind was opened to the conspiracy theory that she was married to Jesus. For many centuries, early Christians revered her as a saint and an example of devotion. By the 13th century, she was referred to as a reformed prostitute that had repented and followed Jesus. Very little is actually mentioned about her in the scriptures. We know she was a devout follower that stayed with him even when the other disciples hid through the Crucifixion, fearing for their own lives.

Mary holds a unique position among the followers and disciples of Jesus. She observed the Crucifixion of our Lord, discovered the empty tomb, and was the first to see him after the Resurrection. In this chapter, you will read her description of these events and what it was like to be in the presence of Jesus.

The eighth chapter of Luke provides some interesting information.

> *Now after this [Jesus] made his way through towns and villages preaching, and proclaiming the Good News of the kingdom of God. With him went the Twelve, as well as certain women who had been cured of evil spirits and ailments: Mary surnamed the Magdalene, from whom seven demons had gone out, Joanna the wife of Herod's steward Chuza, Susanna, and several others who provided for them out of their own resources. (Luke 8:1–3 New Living Translation)*

From that verse, we learn that Mary was cured of evil spirits and that she provided for the other disciples through her resources. No mention is ever made in the gospels that she was a prostitute. The Gnostic gospels, not included in the Bible, add fuel to the fire that Mary and Jesus had a personal relationship. The gospel of Philip states that Jesus kissed Mary on the lips, creating jealousy among the other disciples. A fragment of the gospel of Mary describes her as the woman Jesus loved more than the others. It is interesting to note that these gospels were written many years after the death of Mary.

Message of Mary Magdalene

In December of 2018, the spirit of Mary Magdalene came to us in a channeling session. Here is her message for all of us:

I am here and anxious to speak to all the members of your wonderful group. They represent the best hope for spreading the true words of our Lord. Tonight, let me begin by telling you that evil is spreading and needs to be stopped. Satan has been very, very busy! He has been especially busy in your government and with your enemies that are trying to destroy your country. This needs to stop! God created the United States of America in the image that he wanted for a country. Many have tried to destroy you through the years, and he has always intervened and guided your leaders so that good would always win out in the end. He has seen you through world wars, and he has seen you through a civil war; he has never, ever lost his power for the ability of good to win over evil. Today you are facing a different type of evil. Many of your members of Congress are more interested in their personal power than they are looking out for you, the people. It will be a difficult time in your history, but you must remember the words of Jesus that were spoken, and they apply as much today as they did in the time he walked the earth.

The most important thing for all of you to remember is love for one another. Without that love, hatred will win out, and if hatred wins, your evolution is in question. Tonight, I will answer many questions about my life and about what should take place among mankind. Keep in mind that I am here because Jesus has asked me to come, and he listens as I speak to you. Know that I speak his words, know that Barry and Connie speak his words, and know that the words that you are about to hear are about love and kindness toward one another.

If everyone chooses that love and affection, all will be well. Each of you listening needs to go forth and spread the word of the love of God. It is a very simple message. God does not ever speak of hatred; he only loves each and every one of you and is with each and every one of you; as I said before, it is a very simple message. Each of you needs to remove hatred from your heart; once you accomplish that, it will have a wonderful effect on those around you. Those around you will see the love, and they will chase the hatred from their hearts as well; this is how it will begin. Without that love, all things will end! With that, I am going to answer some questions. Thank you.

Once again, we hear the importance of love.

In the Service of God

The holy spirits are members of the soul family of God and have been serving him for millions of years to have gained such an elevated position in the realms of heaven. I asked Mary if she had ever served God on other planets. Her reply was this:

Yes, as have all of you. We always speak of the influence of God on the other planets in our galaxy. Know that your souls have existed long before humans have walked the earth. The other holy spirits have also brought you the same message.

Indeed, they have! It just is a very difficult concept for humans. Next, I inquired if she had ever served God on Earth before she walked the earth as Mary.

Yes, I had returned at the time of Moses, as did several of the other holy spirits, and we assisted in his journey to bring the Jewish people to safety.

"Will you describe what you were in that lifetime?"

I was a man, and I was very close to Moses. I was one of his assistants. He relied on me to help work with the others, and we had a wonderful relationship.

Several other holy spirits also returned to aid Moses when he led the Israelite people to the Promised Land. All of the great religious events throughout time were aided by the soul family of God.

Life of Mary Magdalene

Since very little is known about the life of Mary, I began by asking if she would tell us about her parents. Her answer was this:

Yes; my parents were relatively wealthy Romans. They had property and lands and were among the upper level of Roman society.

"Can you tell me the names of your parents?"

Yes, my father's name was Amos and my mother's name was Edna.

"Did they have a particular occupation?"

No, they simply were landowners; they had slaves, and they would raise crops and trade them with the other merchants, and that is how they made their money.

"Did you have any brother or sisters?"

Yes, I had two sisters and one brother.

"In what religion were you raised?"

We were raised Jewish; my mother and father were high up in the Jewish faith.

The Bible tells us that Mary was plagued by demons and that Jesus cured her. I inquired if she had any illnesses as a child.

Yes, I had problems; my mind would not let me focus on things. Sometimes I would be unable to speak. In those days, anyone with the mental illness was shunned by the rest of the people. My childhood was very sad because of the way others treated me because of the illness with which I was born.

At least her parents had enough wealth to take care of her. I asked her if she could read or write.

No; because of my illness, I was unable to learn to read and write. I learned after I was cured. I learned to read a few words, but I was never really able to write fluently.

"Did you have an occupation before you met Jesus?"

No; my mental illness did not enable me to ever function in a normal job.

"Were you ever married?"

No, I never married. People with mental illness were not allowed to marry others. After I was cured, I considered marriage, but I was so full of the love of God that I knew my role was to speak his words, so I never married.

Many of the disciples and followers of Jesus sacrificed their personal lives to pursue the teachings of Jesus.

A Miracle Cure

The gospels state that Jesus cured Mary of the "seven devils" that plagued her. I inquired if she had the illness when she first met Jesus. Her reply was this:

Yes; when Jesus met me, I was sitting at the edge of the road, and I was having one of my fits where I was unable to speak. He realized what was happening, he came over, he put his hand upon my head, and he prayed that I would be cured. I immediately began to have a clear mind, I was able to speak normally, and I rose, looked at him, and broke out in tears. When I realized what had happened, I fell down at his feet. He reached down and lifted me up, and the love that I felt when I looked into his eyes was indescribable. I knew at that time that I would have to follow him.

"Was that his first public miracle?"

As far as I know, yes. I know now that I have come home on the other side that he had performed a miracle for his wife before me, but no one ever spoke of that in life. So I believe that I was his first public miracle.

"Did he ask you to join him?"

Yes; he said that I had a love within me that he could feel, and he knew that I would be faithful and that I would be able to follow him, to learn his words, and to speak of him after he was gone.

Whenever we channel with Mary, we can feel her loving energy. Next, I inquired if she was one of the first to join the group of disciples.

Yes, but there were several others before me. John was one of them, but I was really one of the first to join the movement.

"How old were you when you met Jesus?"

I met Jesus when I was around 23 years old.

It is amazing that such a group of young people could change the world.

Following Jesus

Jesus gathered a diversified group of followers that would help him spread the word of the one God. Since Mary was the first among women to follow him, I asked how the other apostles reacted to her joining the group.

At first, they were a bit reluctant because I was a woman; however, once they realized how much I loved our Lord and wanted to assist him, they warmed up to me, and we all became wonderful friends.

"Did other women follow him as well?"

Yes; as the movement grew, both men and women came forward to listen to his preaching and to help spread his words.

"How many women were true followers of Jesus during his lifetime?"

There were five of us by the time of the final meeting on the Mount of Olives. Five of us women were members of the group.

"Will you describe them?"

They were all of poor backgrounds; many, most of them, could neither read nor write, but they truly felt the love of God in their hearts, and they wanted to help this man called Jesus spread the word. They were overcome by his love as well.

It is difficult to imagine the power of Jesus to draw others to him. I asked Mary what it was like to know Jesus in life.

It was an incredible sensation. I cannot describe what it was like to be with him. All he ever did was show love to all of us; he spoke of things that we never heard before, but he spoke simply and directly, and as a result, we came to understand the teaching of the true one God. It was truly an amazing adventure to be with him.

"Mary, what was your role as a disciple?"

My family had wealth, so I helped to fund his mission. Our family money was used to feed and house his followers. As others became involved with him, they also contributed in funds, but I and my family provided the bulk of the funds that were required for him to speak and spread the word.

We had been told before that Mary had funded the expenses of the group. When I asked if she spoke in public during the ministries of Jesus, she replied:

Yes; we would all contribute when he would speak to the people. At times he would speak, and each of us would stand and give testament to the love and understanding that this man had for all that walked the earth.

"Did you have a particular message that you would speak to the people?"

I would generally speak of the love that Jesus had shown to all of us. I would speak that those who showed love in their lives and led good lives would be with our Lord not only on Earth but after they passed. They would be with him in heaven as well.

That certainly was a message that would apply through the ages. Modern fiction has hinted at a personal relationship between Jesus and Mary. I asked her to describe her relationship with Jesus.

I loved him with a true love; we were very close in life. He would talk to me and disclose what he wished to accomplish; he told me that there would be a time that he would leave and that we would have to continue his words, and as a result we would all have a lasting effect upon the world.

"Were you the closest disciple to Jesus?"

I was very close to him, but others were close as well. Peter was very close to him, and Jesus probably told Peter more than he told any of the other disciples.

One of the closest kept secrets of the life of Jesus was the existence of his family. I inquired if Mary ever knew that Jesus was married.

No; he never spoke of him being married or having a family to me in life. Once I returned home here in heaven, I realized that he had been married and with children. Once on this side, I waited until Toba joined us, and I was there to welcome her when she passed.

We were previously told that only Peter was aware that Jesus was married.

The Passing of Jesus

As the end was approaching, Jesus gathered his followers and disciples on the Mount of Olives for his final words and blessings. I asked Mary what it was like to be on the Mount of Olives on that final evening. As she answered, I could feel the emotion in her energy.

He had all of us come together and told us that he would be leaving. He told us that he counted on us to carry on spreading his words. It was a very sad time, and we were all in tears. I was there; all the main disciples were there, as was his mother, Mary, as well. In our hearts, we knew what was going to happen, but we tried, we tried with all our hearts to believe that he would return to us. When the Romans came, it was terrible; they took him, and that was the last we ever got to speak to him.

We have been told that Mary Magdalene and the mother of Jesus were the only ones close to Jesus present at the Crucifixion. I asked if she was present at the end of the life of Jesus.

Yes, Mary and I attended the Crucifixion. The other disciples feared for their lives and were in hiding. We figured that as women we would be safe. So we were there when our Lord drew his final breath. I cannot tell you the grief that overcame Mary and myself; it was a terrible, terrible time!

"Will you tell us the true details about the Crucifixion?"

Yes; our Lord was crucified by himself. There were many Roman soldiers around, but they realized that Jesus was a very special person. They tried to show as much respect as possible while carrying out their orders. Many of the soldiers were in tears as well. When our Lord drew his last breath, many of the solders cried outright. It was a very sad event for all of us. There were no earthquakes, the sky did not darken, and as Matthew was to write, the dead did not rise from the graves. Our Lord died with dignity, and he died quietly. I cannot tell you the absolute grief that we felt.

Much that appears in the Bible about the Crucifixion of Jesus is incorrect. There were only two witnesses to the event, and there were no written documents concerning how Christ died. As time went on, the stories were exaggerated and details added. The gospels tell us that Mary Magdalene was among the women that discovered the empty tomb after Jesus resurrected from the dead. I inquired if she was among the women that discovered the empty tomb.

Yes; we were going to assure that the body of our Lord was properly cared for, but when we arrived at the tomb, the doorway, the stone was moved from the doorway, and the soldiers were around us and asked if we had done it, and I said, "No, we know nothing of this." Perhaps someone had stolen the body of our Lord, but we couldn't understand what was going on. It just added to our grief that we could not prepare the body of Jesus in the proper manner.

"What went through your mind when you saw the tomb was empty?"

We thought somebody stole the body, but we could not figure out why. It was justÉit was terrible! I cannot describe what it was like at that time. Mary was almost hysterical that the body of her son was gone; she, too, had no idea what had happened.

You can just imagine the grief of not finding the body of Jesus without knowing the miracle that had taken place.

Risen from the Dead

Mary had no way of knowing what was about to happen to her, as she was in the depths of despair after observing the death of Jesus and the disappearance of his body from the tomb. The gospels tell us that she was the first to see our Lord after the Resurrection. I asked if she was the first to see him.

Yes; I was blessed in a way no other individual has ever been blessed, to see the presence of our Lord after he rose from the dead.

"What did he say to you when he appeared after the Resurrection?"

He said, "Mary, I want you to spread the word that there is truly life after death, that I have now reappeared, and that you will carry out those words that I have told you in life. You must tell the others! You must explain to them that I have returned as I have prophesized."

It was only at that time that Mary understood that Jesus had told the disciples what would happen after his death. During his lifetime, they never truly understood his words. He had returned to prove that there was life after

Christ's Appearance to Mary Magdalene after the Resurrection – Alexander Ivanov – 1835 – State Russian Museum, St. Petersburg, Russia

death. I inquired what she did to spread the word after the Resurrection. She replied:

For a period of several weeks, Jesus appeared to us on several occasions. It was to convince the rest of the disciples and followers that he truly had risen from the grave and that life was everlasting. I did little for probably three or four months after his death; we grieved so much that he was gone. We prayed to God that he would let him return. Peter in particular thought that God would not take him from us and that he would return, but when we realized that he had truly gone to his home in heaven, we began to set out and speak to others about the miracles we had seen.

Mary Spreads the Words of Jesus

As the reality sank in that Jesus now resided in heaven, the disciples began to speak the words of Jesus and spread his message throughout the known world. I inquired where Mary chose to speak the messages of Jesus.

We all started locally in the Judea area, but as time moved on, many of the disciples went to far parts of our known world at that time and spoke. Many went to Greece, and many went as far as Africa!

It would have been a difficult time for a woman to travel alone through a dangerous world. I asked if she was alone when she began her ministries. Her answer was this:

No, I was accompanied by another follower; his name was Holfil. He was a wonderful person, and he would help protect me as I would speak. He would also speak the words of our Lord, because there were many times that a woman was not accepted in those days.

I could find no information pertaining to the death of Mary Magdalene. When I asked her how she died, the answer was this:

I was martyred. I was actually crucified as was my Lord. I was speaking to a group of my students. I did not realize that my group had been infiltrated by many individuals that did not want the word of God to be spread among the people.

"Where were you killed?"

I was killed in southern Judea.

"Who killed you?"

I was killed by the members of my group. Many of those who I thought were close to me betrayed me. I could not believe what was happening!

"Why were you killed?"

I was killed so that I could no longer spread the words of our Lord. The pagan religion was so deeply ingrained in many of the Romans that to speak against it just infuriated them. As a result, they created great violence against those of us that were trying to speak of the one God.

"How old were you when you were killed?"

I was around 45 years old.

In those days, death was often the reward for spreading the words of God.

From Disciple to Prostitute

It is interesting to note how early Christianity revered Mary as a faithful disciple and the first to see Jesus after the Resurrection. A couple hundred years later, the church altered her reputation to that of a fallen woman, or prostitute. Here is one theory of how that event took place. The Bible refers to the healing of Mary as Jesus removing the seven devils from her. Unfortunately for Mary Magdalene, she had a common first name, and there were several Marys mentioned in the bible. The Gospel of John tells of a Mary, the sister of Martha and Lazarus, that anointed the feet of Jesus. Another woman, a loose-haired prostitute, anoints the feet of Jesus, who forgives her of her sins. In the sixth century, Pope Gregory I became one of the most influential leaders to serve as a pope of the Catholic Church. His writings would become the foundation for future leaders of the church, and this was a time when there was much uncertainty about the true teachings of Jesus. Sadly, for Mary Magdalene, Pope Gregory I became confused about the various Marys and wrote the following:

> *She whom Luke calls the sinful woman, whom John calls Mary, we believe to be the Mary from whom seven devils were ejected according to Mark. And what did these seven devils signify, if not all the vices? The Homily No. 33 of Pope Gregory*

With a stroke of the pen, Mary Magdalene became a woman of ill repute. It should also be noted that this was a time when the role of women in the church was being diminished as well. I asked Mary if she was ever a prostitute.

> *No; that was a story that was made up by the Catholic Church. In the early days, people actually worshipped me as a disciple. There became a time that the church resented the power that women had and their influence. At that time, they made a story that I was a prostitute or a person of ill repute. I never, never did what the church blamed me for.*

She is hinting that Pope Gregory I may have had an ulterior motive in reducing her stature in the church. Even today she is thought of by many as a repentant sinner.

Life in Heaven

Now that the soul of Mary Magdalene is in heaven, she serves our Lord from the highest realm. I inquired if she had ever reincarnated since she walked the earth with Jesus.

> *No; since I walked the earth with our Lord, I have served him from heaven.*

"Do you intend to reincarnate in the future?"

If our Lord requests that I return, I would certainly not hesitate to do so.

It would be hard to turn down a specific request of Jesus. I always try to ask the spirits to describe heaven for us. Here is her description:

I will try. It is the place of unimaginable beauty! It is a place of love! There is no evil over here; when you obtain the upper levels of heaven, it is truly beyond your imagination. You can imagine you want to be somewhere, and you will be there; you can visit places, you can do what you wish to do—it is such a wonderful place. No one should ever fear death, because it is the doorway to returning home to all the wonders that surround us here every day.

Once again, we hear that death is not the end but the beginning of a new cycle of life.

The Lost Gospel of Mary

The papyrus containing the lost Gospel of Mary was discovered in the late 19th century near Akhmim in Upper Egypt. It was purchased by a German scholar in 1896 and taken to Berlin for study. The surviving manuscript is missing pages 1 to 6 and pages 11 to 14. The ancient book was probably bound in the late fourth or early fifth century, but the original text was probably written in Greek during the second century. It is considered a Gnostic gospel. Since Mary could neither read nor write, her book had to be written from what was remembered of her words. I inquired if she would tell us some of the information that was lost in her gospel. Her answer was this:

My gospel was written by others; it was based on what I taught when I spoke as I tried to spread the words of our Lord. It spoke of the truth of his death, and it spoke of the wonderful sensation to be the first to see him. Imagine being chosen to be the first to see our Lord after he reappeared! There are also parts that spoke of the other disciples and how they felt about one another.

There is an interesting portion in chapter 9 of her gospel that discusses the opinion of the other disciples when Mary described what she witnessed after the Resurrection:

When Mary had said this, she fell silent, since it was to this point that the Savior had spoken with her. But Andrew answered and said to the brethren, Say what you wish to say about what she has said. I at least do not believe that the Savior said this. For certainly these teachings are strange ideas. Peter answered and spoke concerning these same things. He questioned them about the Savior: Did He really speak privately with a woman and not openly to us? Are we to turn about and all listen to her? Did He prefer her to us? Then Mary wept and said to Peter, My brother Peter, what do you think? Do you think that I have thought this up myself in my heart, or that I am lying about the Savior? Levi answered and said to Peter, Peter you have always been hot tempered. Now I see you contending against the woman like the adversaries. But if the Savior made her worthy, who are you indeed to reject her? Surely the Savior knows her very well. That is why He loved her more than us. Rather let us be ashamed and put on the perfect Man, and separate as He commanded us and preach the gospel, not laying down any other rule or other law beyond what the Savior said. (Mary 9:1–9, The Gospel of Mary Magdalene, Translated by GEORGE W. MACRAE and R. McL. WILSON Edited by DOUGLAS M. PARROTT)

Judging from the text of her gospel, her words were not always accepted because of her sex. My next question addressed whether any of the lost information in her original gospel would ever be found. Her reply was this:

Sadly, there was only a single copy that remains. Keep in mind that the Romans decreed that the gospels be destroyed. Luckily mine was hidden, but portions of it are gone forever.

“Who wrote your gospel?”

Part of it was written by the individual that accompanied me on my mission, Holfil, and part of it was written by others of the disciples that could read and write. I know that Paul contributed some to what was written in my lost gospel.

It is a sad fact that much of her gospel is lost to the ages.

Opinions and Messages of Mary Magdalene

As we neared the end of our interview, I began to ask her advice on current events and how to handle resistance to our work in spreading the contemporary words of our Lord. I asked her for a recommendation on what to tell those that say what we are doing is against biblical teachings, to be communicating with spirits.

If it were against biblical teachings, I would not be here with you tonight. It may be against what is written in the Bible, but it is certainly not against what Jesus wants for all of us. He wishes that humans can communicate with him to understand his preachings and to understand the love he has for all. You and Connie were sent back to communicate with us. You are now capable of speaking the words not only of Jesus but of his followers, such as myself and the other disciples. It is only through communication with the holy spirits that others can be told the truth. The Bible is but a guide; man has influenced the words that are in the Bible for their own power and strength. For instance, what they wrote about me is the greatest example: I was never a prostitute; I never considered it! There was no need! My family had money! Luckily, they took care of me until our Lord healed me, but what they added about me was a sin. It is the responsibility of all of you that you can hear the truth of his words and to pass on these words and to let others know that Barry and Connie can speak of the truth. Do not fear what others say; they are wrong! Once they arrive over here, they will learn of their mistake.

At the time I wrote this chapter, a large caravan of individuals from Central America were attempting to enter our country. I asked her opinion of what was taking place on our Mexican border.

What is taking place is terrible for many aspects. It is imperative that the United States be protected. If your country does not survive, there will be no one else to provide world leadership. It is important that the integrity of your country be protected, but on the other hand, we feel for the poor people that are trying to come into your country. They are being misled, and those that are misleading them are creating a terrible sin. Sadly, the people attempting to come into your country are paying the price for the greed and hatred of others. Your country must enforce its borders! Sadly, there are those that are trying to replace your borders. For your country to remain strong, there must be safety for all in your country, and to do that, a country must have strong borders.

"Do you have a message for Connie and me?"

Yes; once again, you are speaking the words of spirits from the other side that have followed our Lord in life. You have been sent back to do this, and you are accomplishing what you have been sent back to do. It is important that others learn to communicate with us as well. There will be a time that you and Connie will no longer be able to do this; others must speak of your legacy, and others must also learn to communicate with us and to lead other people to the true teachings and words of our Lord. For the time being, you and Connie will bring the majority of the messages to the people. When your book comes out this fall, others will have the information they need to speak the truth of the life of our Lord. I've contributed to that book, as you know; hopefully many will read the book and understand the wonderful, simple story of the life of Jesus.

Mary was referring to my last book, *Spirits Speak: Channeling the Life of Jesus*. It laid the foundation for a lot of the information presented in this book. In my final question, I inquired if she had a final message for members of our Facebook group, Words of God Then and Now.

Yes; you have been brought together to go forth and spread the words as they are given to you by Barry and Connie; they speak the truth. I know that there are many doubters out there. There were many doubters when I walked the earth with

Jesus; there are also many haters, because they cannot stand to hear the truth. You have to attempt to bring people together; once you accomplish this, you will have done what you were sent back to do. With those words, I am going to leave you tonight. God bless all of you; Jesus has been here with me and has been listening, and he is well pleased with the messages that I have given you. I have spoken the truth! I have spoken the truth as only one who is near to Jesus can speak. Go forth and spread his words! Go forth and spread his love! Go forth and tell others that hatred has no place in heaven; those that live a life of hatred will not advance in realms of his kingdom. God bless all of you, and good night!

God has certainly blessed the spirit of Mary Magdalene!

CHAPTER 7

Saint Peter, the Right Hand of Jesus

Anyone that has ever opened the Bible is familiar with the name of Saint Peter. It is written that he and his brother Andrew became some of the early disciples of Jesus. We are told that he was the leader of the disciples and acted as their spokesperson, yet as an example of human frailty, when questioned by the Romans if he knew Jesus, he disavowed him. He was also known as Simon Peter, and we are told many things in the gospels about his calling and his brutal martyrdom. The Catholic Church considers him the first pope. His words are quoted in many of the gospels, and he was the leader of the apostles. One evening, we were honored to interview the spirit of Saint Peter in a live internet session.

A Message from Peter

I began the session by asking if he had a message for our listeners.

> *I am here tonight to bring you the words of our Lord. When Jesus walked the earth, he spoke of love and devotion to the one God. To know Jesus was to know pure love! All that he did was to show how much God loved humans. When he was crucified, he rose again from the dead. His Resurrection was the greatest miracle of all times. When Jesus rose from the dead, he proved that the power of God is great! As we gather here tonight, we all should accept the miracle of what is happening. I am here as part of that miracle! As the days progress, more and more will happen to show you the power of God. As we move forward in spreading his words, all will come to realize that what you are watching is very real. Soon all must stand to preach his words, or Satan will overcome all. God is love, and those who speak his*

words will join him in the realms of heaven. Yes, we are all blessed to hear these words; now I will answer your questions.

As you can see, his spirit is still as fervent in preaching the words of God as he was in life. I asked if he preferred if we call him Peter or Simon Peter. He replied:

Peter is fine.

I was humbled by the fact that we were on a first-name basis with one that sits at the right hand of our Lord.

His Life

It is written that he and his brother Andrew were fishermen. I verified that Andrew was his brother.

Yes.

The Tears of Saint Peter – El Greco – cc1590 – Museo Soumaya, Mexico City, Mexico.

In our earlier session with John the Baptist, we learned that he played a larger role in bringing people to follow Jesus than I had realized. My next question addressed whether his brother Andrew was a follower of John the Baptist.

He knew of John the Baptist, that is how Andrew grew to know God.

"How did you meet Jesus?"

I was introduced by Andrew.

"How old were you when you met Jesus?"

Twenty-three.

"What was your occupation when you first met Jesus?"

A fisherman and a carpenter.

He was verifying the information recorded in the gospels about his life. My research had not disclosed much about his personal life, so I asked if he was married.

Yes; my wife's name was Esther.

"Did you have any children?"

Yes, we had four children.

Once again, we see that these young men relinquished married lives and family to follow the teachings of Jesus and convert citizens to the one God. They were surely aware of the risks they would be taking by opposing the pagan worship of the Romans. The brutality of King Herod the Great and his son Herod Antipas must have been fresh in their minds. Next, I inquired if Peter had the ability to read and write. He answered:

Somewhat; I tried to learn to write, but I was too busy spreading the words of God.

"Were you able to draft any of your own gospels?"

I tried but was not proficient enough in writing. I told my stories to others, and they wrote of my words.

He was incapable of recording his own words, so any writings about him would have been done by others. Notes were not taken during the events of his lifetime, and what is said to have been his words would have been taken from stories told by others. I began by asking, "Where did you live when you first met Jesus?"

Galilee.

All of the disciples and followers came from the same general area.

Meeting Our Lord

"When you first met Jesus, did you know that he was God incarnate?"

No; I thought he was the Son of God but came to realize that he really was God incarnate.

"Were you the first ordained apostle?"

No; that would have been Andrew.

"Did Jesus perform any kind of act or miracle to convince you to leave your family and follow him?"

No; I knew from my brother and John the Baptist who he was.

John the Baptist played an immense role in launching the ministries of Jesus. He had truly been sent back by God to prepare the way for the ministries of Jesus. "Who were the apostles closest to Jesus?"

I was probably the closest to him, but there were others.

"Who were the other disciples and followers that were closest to Jesus?"

Mary, John, and Matthew were very close.

His mentioning that Mary Magdalene was very close to Jesus reminded me that some of the other gospels not included in the Bible indicated that there were times that Peter resented the presence of Mary. I asked him of his opinion of Mary Magdalene.

She was a trusted disciple and follower of our Lord. There were times I resented her because I felt Jesus was favoring her, but he was only shielding her from the resentment of her being a female. Mary and I are very close over here.

Even among those chosen to walk with Jesus, there was apparently jealousy among them. We have been told many times that the followers and disciples still work very hard to influence humans to follow the words of God. I thought I would inquire what Jesus taught his disciples, so I asked if he ever talked of reincarnation.

Yes, he told all of the followers of reincarnation.

As I have mentioned many times, reincarnation is the product of the everlasting life of the soul. Having written two books about aliens, I asked if Jesus ever spoke of life on other planets.

Yes; he spoke of the power of God throughout the universe and that others followed him on other worlds.

That had to be very hard to understand. "Did he ever speak to you of his family?"

He only told me that he was married and had children. It was very important that the secret was kept, protecting his family.

"After Jesus was crucified, did you ever meet his family?"

No; I did not want to endanger them.

It was critical to Jesus that his family was protected. Because of that protection, there are many people walking the earth today that are descendants of Jesus. It is widely written that Peter was the main spokesman for the apostles.

I asked if he really was the spokesman for the followers and apostles. His answer was this:

Yes; our Lord entrusted me with being spokesman.

"How were you selected to be the first among his followers?"

I always had the complete trust of our Lord Jesus. It just naturally happened that I assumed the role of leader. Others also had important roles.

Much of the writings about Peter focus on the events prior to the Crucifixion and after the Resurrection. I asked him how many years he knew Jesus before he was crucified. He answered:

Four.

That meant that the leader of the disciples was around 27 years old at the time of the death of Jesus.

Death and Resurrection

I asked if Jesus ever confided in him that our Lord was approaching the end of his life. Peter replied:

Yes; he warned us that he would soon be leaving and that we would have to carry on his words. It was terribly sad for all of us.

"Did Jesus tell you that there would be a time that you would renounce him?"

Yes; I hate that he knew the truth.

"Did you renounce Jesus?"

Yes; I lacked the courage that he had.

"Did Jesus ever speak of you renouncing him to any of the other followers?"

No, he only told me.

Jesus knew in advance the events that were to result in his death. On the evening that Judas betrayed Jesus, it is written that Peter drew his sword and cut off the ear of a soldier in an attempt to defend our Lord. I asked if he cut off the ear as written in the gospels.

Yes; I was attempting to protect our Lord, but he told me to stop. He knew it was his time and nothing should be done to interfere.

"Did Jesus perform a miracle and replace the ear of the soldier?"

Yes; it was his last miracle.

"When Jesus was taken, did you go to the temple of the high priest?"

No; I was afraid for my life. I regret being a coward.

In my opinion, one of the most important traits of Jesus was to recognize the human frailties of others and to forgive them. Despite Peter fearing for his own life while Jesus knew his life was about to end, our Lord also realized that Peter would play an enormous role in the future, bringing individuals to worship the one God. All of the followers and disciples, with the exception of Mary Magdalene, hid to protect their own lives during the trials and the Crucifixion of Jesus.

We are told in the gospels that Peter was the first of the male disciples to visit the tomb of Jesus and find that it was empty. When I asked him if he was the first to witness the event, he replied:

Yes; I thought someone had stolen his body. I did not realize the miracle that was happening before my eyes.

"Who was the first apostle to see the risen Jesus?"

Mary was the first.

"Did he appear to you?"

Yes, he appeared to me soon after I realized the tomb was empty.

"How many times did he appear to you?"

Three.

"Did you believe that God would return Jesus to Earth to complete his ministries?"

Yes; I thought the work of our Lord was not complete and that God would perform a miracle and return him.

It is difficult to imagine the incredible love the followers of Jesus felt for him. It must have seemed that life was unimaginable without him.

Life after Jesus

After Jesus appeared to Peter, he spread the words of God in many areas of the Middle East. Many of the apostles were given the gift of healing to demonstrate the powers of God and to provide proof of his powers. I asked Peter if he ever personally performed any miracles. He replied:

Yes; I had the ability to heal others to prove the powers of God, just as you will have that ability.

"Did you ever try to walk on water?"

Yes, but I failed.

Jesus also told us that he failed to walk on water, so it does not surprise me that Peter would suffer the same results. It is written in the gospels that Herod Agrippa had Peter jailed but an angel intervened and helped him escape. I asked him if he was imprisoned by Herod Agrippa. Peter replied:

Yes.

"How did you get out of prison?"

I was released because Agrippa feared riots.

"The gospels state that an angel helped you escape from prison."

No, that was made up later.

Death of Peter

The Bible does not tell us how Peter died, but it is generally accepted by the church that he was crucified upside down on an inverted cross because he did not consider himself worthy to die in the same manner as Jesus. I started to inquire about his death by asking how old he was when he died.

Sixty-five.

"How did you die?"

I was not crucified.

So much for the traditional story of his death. I restated the question by stating that the traditional story is that he was crucified upside down. He answered:

I know, but that is not true.

"How did you die?"

I died of illness.

"So you died a natural death?"

Yes.

I guess dying a natural death would not be something to be remembered. Roman Emperor Nero is often blamed for having Peter martyred. I asked him if the story of Nero having him killed was made up in the gospels.

Correct.

Nero is blamed for a lot of evil events, but I guess we will let him off the hook on this one. It is also stated that Peter died on the 10th anniversary of Nero's reign. He answered:

No. They later wanted it to appear I was martyred, and they actually buried my body with the other martyrs.

"Were you buried in the area where St. Peter's Basilica now stands?"

Yes, I was buried there.

"Are your bones on display in a niche of the graffiti wall?"

Yes, but there are others there as well.

"Many consider you the first pope of the Catholic Church. Do you believe that to be true?"

Many believe that, but I never held that role.

"What is your opinion of the current Catholic Church?"

The current church has lost its true identity with our Lord. The primary force should be the love of God and leading a life following his commands and not the primary love of the church.

Although the words of Peter appear in many places in the Bible, his own gospels were not selected. I asked him in what gospels his words appeared, and he replied:

Matthew, Mark, Luke, John, and portions of others.

A fragment of the Gospel of Peter was discovered in 1884 in Egypt. It describes the passion of Christ and exonerates Pontius Pilate. Translations of the portions of the Gospel of Peter can be readily accessed on the internet. I asked Peter what he considered the most important part of his gospel. He answered:

I tell of the dignity of our Lord on the cross. He maintained pride until the end.

That is exactly what we had been told before about the Crucifixion of Jesus. I asked how accurate to his original words he considered the words of his gospel.

Parts have been altered by the church for power.

Once again, we are told that the original words of the apostles and Jesus have been altered through time and will never be really known. I inquired if it was appropriate for individuals to pray to the saints as well as God for guidance.

Yes; I welcome their prayers and hear each and every one of them. All should pray to our Lord and also his disciples and followers. They will listen and guide you.

We have been told many times that each and every prayer is heard, not only by God but by other holy spirits.

Advice of Peter

While we were blessed with the presence of Peter, I asked if he could give guidance into the best way to engage others to believe the contemporary words we are receiving of the holy spirits and Jesus. He responded:

> *We faced the same challenges. It will not be easy. You must start by having simple conversation and invite others to view these miracles. Things will happen in the future to make your mission easier. As Barry's books become available, you will all have the contemporary information available. Learn of what we speak and listen closely to the messages of the holy spirits and our Lord.*

It is comforting to know that we are facing the same challenges as those faced by the original apostles and followers of Jesus 2,000 years ago. I guess not much has changed through the years. I find it hard to believe that we are the only individuals in this entire world that are blessed to receive these contemporary messages of faith. I asked Peter if there were other individuals or religions receiving similar messages. He answered:

> *Yes; we are trying to spread his words in many ways. Others also receive messages, but Barry and Connie have a very special role.*

We have been told that on numerous occasions, but Connie and I still find it hard to believe what is happening. We have developed a group of very devout followers on social media and other places. I asked Peter if the other people are being taken as seriously as the people that are following our messages.

> *Some, but it is very difficult.*

I can certainly concur with that statement. You would think that if people were given the opportunity to hear actual messages from Jesus and the saints, they would open their minds and at least approach their messages with an open mind. I asked Saint Peter if he had a final message for the individuals hearing his words.

Yes; go with the blessings of our Lord and God. He will watch over all of you listening and viewing tonight. God bless everyone! Amen!

The message of Saint Peter was an inspiration to Connie and me. His energy was that of one that was close to God, and he spoke in a forceful and knowledgeable manner. His presence was truly a miracle. We had been honored to be in the presence of the spirit that was the closest to Jesus when he walked the earth.

CHAPTER 8

Saint Matthew

Anyone that has ever opened the Bible is familiar with the name Matthew. You will find his name as the title of the first book of the collection of gospels known as the New Testament. In reality, very little is known about the man known as Saint Matthew. It is not even verified that he is the author of the gospel that bears his name. We are told that he was a tax collector and Jesus invited him to become a follower. It is also written that he became one of the 12 disciples and a member of the inner circle of Jesus.

While he is mentioned in multiple books of the New Testament, little is told about his life and his relationship with Jesus. There is no mention of where he taught or even how he died.

A Message from Matthew

In October of 2018, we were blessed with his presence in a channeling session that we conducted on Facebook Live for all to see. He began the session with the following message:

> *I am excited to be able to speak to the people once more about my love of God and what it was like to know our Lord Jesus. I want all of you here tonight to understand that it is really my spirit present with you and speaking with you through Barry and Connie. God is always with you; never doubt that! There are times of darkness in all of your lives. When I was alive as Matthew, I went through periods*

of depression and sadness, but once I met our Lord Jesus the Christ, my life became fulfilled. There were still many instances of pain and suffering for me, but I then knew that all would be well and I would reside in heaven with our Lord. It was a difficult time; the Romans were brutal and would not hesitate to torture and crucify any that spoke against their rule. We were introducing a unique concept to them, and their leaders highly resented it.

Today there is much evil as well. Your government is trying to take God away from you, and they are succeeding. You were sent back to Earth as a tool to defeat that trend. You must be strong in the face of all that is going on around you. One major problem is the growth of abortion. Abortion is taking a life, and that is a sin. While there may be circumstances that make it a forgivable sin, it is nonetheless a sin. No one protects the small child being carried by the mother except the mother and its family. It is up to all to end the killing of the innocents. Many in political office feel that such killing is justified. They will find out when they arrive back home that it was very much against the teachings of our Lord and God. We are proud of what you are accomplishing at the present time; soon much will happen. When the book arrives about the life and preaching of our Lord, he will make it much easier to spread his words. You are among the chosen ones to bring the love of God back to this world. There will be a time that Barry and Connie will no longer be able to bring you our messages. It is important that those of you that have the ability to communicate with us do so; that will allow our messages to continue. Barry and Connie will try their best to teach others how to receive our messages. With that, I am ready to answer questions.

Truly a wonderful and inspiring message! One subject that is reoccurring among the saints is their hatred of abortion and the killing of innocents.

Matthew Answers Questions about His Life

As I have mentioned many times, the energy of the soul is eternal, and that soul energy is the everlasting life taught by our Lord. Reincarnation is the key to the soul advancing in heaven, and the history of the soul predates the time humans have walked the earth. I began by asking Matthew if he ever served our Lord in lifetimes before he walked the earth as Matthew. He replied:

Yes, I was present in prior lifetimes on Earth.

Having written extensively about lifetimes before humans were present on Earth, I inquired if he ever served God on other planets. As anticipated, the answer was this:

Of course, as did all of you.

That is a difficult concept for many, but it is true that we have all been on other planets in other, earlier lifetimes. Getting back to his lifetime as Matthew, I asked where he was born.

I was born in Judea, near the shores of Galilee.

What was your given name in that lifetime?

I was known as Ethan.

That answer is in contrast to what is surmised by religious scholars. They believe his given name was Levi. "How did you get the name Matthew?"

Once I became a follower of Jesus, we assumed names other than those in which we were born for the protection of our families.

"Were you raised in any religion?"

Yes, I was raised in the pagan religions of the Romans. I had heard of the one God but felt the old ways were better.

"Did you have any brother or sisters?"

Yes, I had two sisters and one brother.

"Did any of them follow Jesus?"

No, they remained in the pagan religion.

"What was your education?"

My family was well-to-do and had me educated so that I could read and write.

During this period of time, one of the most hated occupations was that of being a tax collector. It is written in the gospels that Matthew was a tax collector when he chose to follow Jesus. I inquired why he became a tax collector.

While the profession was hated by most, it was the best way to gain power with the Romans.

When Jesus began his ministries, Galilee was ruled by Herod Antipas, the son of the cruel Herod the Great that attempted to kill the baby Jesus. I asked Matthew his opinion of Herod Antipas.

He was far more inclined to be fair than his father. Herod the Great was sent to the lower level, but his son Antipas was not sent there; he remains in heaven.

In those days, it would have been highly unlikely for a person with such a lucrative job as tax collector to quit and follow an individual teaching a religion in total contrast to the Roman way of thinking. I inquired how he came to follow Jesus.

I was told about the man who spoke of the one God. I was working when Jesus and a few of his followers approached me. I could feel the loving energy that he radi-

ated. I knew immediately that he was very special and that I wanted to become one with him.

"How old were you when you decided to follow Jesus?"

I was 25.

"Did someone introduce you to Jesus?"

No; he approached me and spoke of the one God and asked if I would join him.

"What was it like to be in the presence of Jesus?"

All you would feel was the love radiating from him; it is difficult to describe the incredible feeling of being with our Lord. I never saw him angry with any of us. He always spoke softly and would tell us what he expected of us.

One can only imagine what it is like to be in his presence. We were told earlier that Jesus kept the existence of his family a secret for their safety. I verified that by asking if he ever met the family of Jesus during his lifetime as Matthew.

No; I never knew he was married until I came home. Once I was back in heaven, I was introduced to the soul of Toba, who was his wife. After his children came home, I met them as well.

They all refer to heaven as the true home for your soul. We have been told that there were as many as 45 followers of Jesus; the gospels refer to there being 12 that were in his inner circle and most trusted. I inquired how he was selected as one of the members of the inner circle of Jesus.

There were actually more than 12 highly trusted disciples. I tried my best to gain the confidence of our Lord. He realized I was truly committed to following him and carrying on his mission.

"What was your role when you were among the other disciples?"

I would help with the finances, since I had been trained in addition and subtraction. That was required to be a tax collector.

"What was your opinion of Mary Magdalene?"

I loved Mary both when we walked the earth and now that we are together in heaven. She was instrumental in providing funds to support the ministry. She was highly trusted by our Lord.

Events around the Death of Jesus

The gospel of Matthew describes the death of Jesus as follows:

From noon until three in the afternoon darkness came over all the land. About three in the afternoon Jesus cried out in a loud voice, "Eli, Eli, lema sabachthani?" (which means "My God, my God, why have you forsaken me?"). When some of those standing there heard this, they said, "He's calling Elijah." Immediately one of them ran and got a sponge. He filled it with wine vinegar, put it on a staff, and offered it to Jesus to drink. The rest said, "Now leave him alone. Let's see if Elijah comes to save him." And when Jesus had cried out again in a loud voice, he gave up his spirit. At that moment the curtain of the temple was torn in two from top to bottom. The earth shook, the rocks split and the tombs broke open. The bodies of many holy people who had died were raised to life. They came out of the tombs after Jesus' resurrection and went into the holy city and appeared to many people. (Matthew 27:45–53 New International Version)

We have been told earlier that the disciples feared for their safety and were in hiding during the Crucifixion of Jesus. I inquired who told him of the details of the Crucifixion that were included in the gospel named after him.

Unfortunately, I acted cowardly and hid during the Crucifixion of our Lord; only the two Marys were present when he passed from the earth. They told us what happened. After time passed, many others tried to give us details about his passing; many were inaccurate, and unfortunately some of those words were included in the gospels.

"Did you witness the Resurrection?"

I saw the body of our Lord after the Resurrection, but I was not among the first to see him.

"How many times did you see Jesus after the Resurrection?"

Twice.

We are told in Acts 1:6–12 that after speaking to his disciples, he ascended into heaven. Here is the biblical description:

Then they gathered around him and asked him, "Lord, are you at this time going to restore the kingdom to Israel?" He said to them: "It is not for you to know the times or dates the Father has set by his own authority. But you will receive power when the Holy Spirit comes on you; and you will be my witnesses in Jerusalem, and in all Judea and Samaria, and to the ends of the earth." After he said this, he was taken up before their very eyes, and a cloud hid him from their sight. They were looking intently up into the sky as he was going, when suddenly two men dressed in white stood beside them. "Men of Galilee," they said, "why do you stand here looking into the sky? This same Jesus, who has been taken from you into heaven, will come back in the same way you have seen him go into heaven." Then the apostles returned to Jerusalem from the hill called the Mount of Olives, a Sabbath day's walk from the city. (NIV)

I asked Matthew if he witnessed the ascension of Jesus into heaven. He answered:

No; there was no ascension. That was added to the gospels at a later time.

Once again, we see that the truth got a little help through the years.

Matthew Spreads the Words of Jesus

Upon the death of Jesus, his followers spread out across the known world to tell others of his words. Little is known about the life of Matthew after the passing of Christ. I inquired if he preached in Judea.

I did for a time, but I decided to travel and try to speak his words in other countries.

"How long did you remain in Judea?"

I stayed about three years after his passing, but then I began my travels.

"Where did you go when you left Judea?"

I decided that no one was going to try to spread his words in Africa, so I began to head in that direction.

"Did you ever go to Ethiopia?"

Yes, I wound up there, but it was very difficult to spread his words in that country.

Any travel in those days was extremely difficult and dangerous. I asked Matthew if anyone accompanied him in his travels. His reply was this:

Yes; there were several other followers that accompanied me and supported me in spreading his words.

"In what countries did you wind up teaching?"

I spoke in Egypt and in what is now Ethiopia.

"In life, what was the message that you preached?"

I spoke of the love of the one God. I spoke that what the Romans were practicing was not what would help the soul to go to heaven. I taught that each must love one another. That is what Jesus taught, and it is still a most important message today.

"Did you preach that the Messiah would return?"

Yes, because I felt that God would send him back to us. I was wrong in that teaching; I missed him so much that I thought surely that God would intervene and return him to us.

The death of Jesus was heart-wrenching for his followers. I could find no writings describing the death of Matthew. I asked him in what country he died.

I died in Ethiopia.

"How did you die?"

I was crucified by the Romans in that country. They warned me that I would not be welcomed with my preaching. I still spoke of the one God and the love of our Lord.

The disciples' love of God and desire to spread his words overcame any fear of death. I inquired at what age he was crucified.

Fifty-four.

Martyrdom of Saint Matthew – Caravaggio – 1600 – San Luigi dei Francesi, Rome, Italy

I read that the relics of the life of Saint Matthew were stored in the city of Naddaver in Ethiopia. They were transferred to Salerno, Italy, in the year AD 954, where they were kept in a cave for protection. The Salerno Cathedral houses a crypt that is said to hold his remains. I asked him if any relics of his lifetime currently exist. He replied:

No; what is said to have been mine is false.

There are a lot of people in Salerno that are not going to like that answer.

The Gospels of Matthew

There is no proof that the gospel named after Matthew was really authored by the Saint. Much of what we know about Jesus was based on stories and hearsay. Since he could read and write, I asked him if he took notes while he was a follower of Jesus. His response was this:

Yes; I tried to record some of what he spoke and my experiences as I traveled, trying to spread his words.

"Were those notes used in your gospel?"

Some, but much was distorted through the years.

Sadly, that is what we are told about much of the information in the Bible. Men could not resist the urge to manipulate the wording to strengthen their powers. I asked how his notes compared to what is written in his gospel.

That is a difficult question. I would estimate that perhaps half of what is written is accurate.

"Do you consider your gospel authentic?"

In part; for instance, the death of our Lord was based on stories told to me. Unfortunately, some of those stories were not accurate. When our Lord passed, the sky did not darken, and there were no earthquakes. The dead did not rise from the grave. Mary told us that he passed with dignity. I should not have paid attention to the other stories.

"What do you consider the greatest error in your gospel?"

What I just told you.

"Did you write any gospels that were not included in the Bible?"

Yes; I contributed to many other gospels, but they were not included.

Sadly, much of the truth about the life of our Lord was either lost or distorted through the years. I inquired if there was anything in his lifetime as Matthew that he regretted.

I regret that I was a coward and hid during the Crucifixion of our Lord. If I had that to do over, I would have taken my chances with the two Marys. I learned when I arrived home that my mission was to live and pass on his words. Had I gone to the Crucifixion, I would probably have been arrested and suffered the same fate as our Lord.

Once again, we see how events are preordained in heaven.

Home in Heaven

We have been told that heaven is not in the sky, but it is the sky. Heaven is all around us, just in another dimension. I asked Saint Matthew if he would describe heaven for us.

It is impossible to describe the grandeur of heaven. When you are on the upper realms, there is no limit to the wonders. Life on the middle realms is also magnificent. You have free will to travel as you please and visit those who are in your level or below you. You will join your soul family, and it will be a wonderful reunion. When you and Connie pass, you will be met by your family and those of us that are available. You will be allowed to spend some time with your family before returning to the upper level that is your home.

"What is your current role in heaven?"

I assist our Lord with trying to spread words of his love. It is becoming more difficult to accomplish anything from over here. Satan has exerted his influence on men. That is why you were sent back!

"When Connie and I are on the other side, do we know your soul?"

> *Of course; we are all together over here, serving our Lord. You and Connie have been sent back many times to spread his words.*

We have been told many times that there are seven realms in heaven, with God in the highest realm. In addition, there is a lower realm where those souls that carry out unforgivable sins are sent to be rehabilitated. Having never really understood how the lower realm fit into the picture, I inquired if the lower realm was really the first realm of heaven. His response was this:

> *No; there are seven realms besides that lower realm.*

"Have you ever reincarnated since your life as Matthew?"

> *Yes; I returned during the Inquisition to try to bring reason to the church. Satan was too strong, and I failed.*

"Are you planning to reincarnate again?"

> *I will when our Lord asks me to do so, just as you and Connie have responded to his request.*

Souls are asked to serve our Lord in many ways, either through incarnate lives or as soul energies on the other side.

Current Events

In the fall of 2018, when I wrote this chapter, hatred was rampant in the United States, and the Catholic Church was being torn apart with molestation charges. I asked Matthew to give his advice for pushing back against hatred in the world today. His answer was this:

> *You must speak to others of love! Start by telling those with problems that God is always with them and will see them through their difficulties if they give him a*

chance. Speak of the love that all of you feel for each other. Speak of the love that God feels for all, even the sinners. Speak of forgiveness, for God will forgive those who find his love in their hearts. I am an example. I was a sinner, and God forgave me. I was not perfect, but God forgave me. None of you are perfect, and God will forgive you as well.

"What is your opinion on what is happening in our current times on Earth?"

We are saddened by the growth of Satan and especially as reflected in the abortion of the unborn. Now is the time that you must all take firm actions and defeat the evil. The evolution of humans depends upon it. God will not look favorably upon humans if the wholesale slaughter of babies in the womb and the atheistic teachings are allowed to continue.

Saint Matthew is one of the most renowned of the Catholic saints. He is celebrated worldwide. I asked him his opinion of the current Catholic Church.

It saddens me to think of what has become of my church. The cruelty to others, especially the young, is breaking our hearts. Those that perform those cruel acts will be dealt with when they arrive over here. There will be a time that the Catholic Church rebuilds and becomes one with the teachings of our Lord.

That opinion is reflected by all of the holy spirits that have been asked the question.

Messages of Saint Matthew

Throughout our interview with Matthew, I was impressed with his strong energy and frankness in his answers. I inquired if he had any messages for members of our Facebook group, Words of God Then and Now.

Yes; know that they are here to assist you in your mission. You will find support for your mission in unexpected places. There is nowhere that we will not be to assist you. God knows how important it is that you find the strength to defeat Satan today. Just remember that God is love, God is with you, and God will forgive you of your sins. With those messages in your heart, you will not fail.

"Do you have a final message for us tonight?"

> *Yes; tonight was a special experience for me. I got to tell others of the love of God. Now it is up to you to repeat those words and show that you are modern disciples of our Lord and Messiah. Keep in mind, God will always win. In the face of God, Satan will shrink and be gone. We are with you always, and you are with us as well. When you come home, you will realize the wonderful job that you have done. Go in peace, and God bless you all! Thank you for listening to me tonight.*

We were truly blessed to be able to bring you the inspiring interview with Saint Matthew.

CHAPTER 9

Saint Timothy

Saint Timothy was not a member of the original disciples and followers that walked with Jesus. He was brought to the calling of the one God by Saint Paul the Apostle after the Resurrection of our Lord. His main contributions to the Bible are the gospels First and Second Timothy, which basically consist of letters of instruction. In 1 Timothy, 1:12–17, we are given insight into his recorded teachings through the words of the Apostle Paul:

> *I thank Christ Jesus our Lord, who has strengthened me, because He considered me faithful, putting me into service, even though I was formerly a blasphemer and a persecutor and a violent aggressor. Yet I was shown mercy because I acted ignorantly in unbelief; and the grace of our Lord was more than abundant, with the faith and love which are found in Christ Jesus. It is a trustworthy statement, deserving full acceptance, that Christ Jesus came into the world to save sinners, among whom I am foremost of all. Yet for this reason I found mercy, so that in me as the foremost, Jesus Christ might demonstrate His perfect patience as an example for those who would believe in Him for eternal life. Now to the King eternal, immortal, invisible, the only God, be honor and glory forever and ever. Amen. (New International Version)*

In November of 2018, we were blessed with the presence of the spirit of Saint Timothy for an interview on Facebook Live.

Good evening, I am pleased to be here tonight. This is a great opportunity for me to once again speak the words of our Lord. This may perhaps be the largest audience that I have ever spoken to. It is certainly the largest audience I have spoken to for several thousand years. I want all of you to know that Jesus is here with us tonight and is also listening and that he blesses each and every one of you and thanks you for listening.

Tonight I want to speak about the hatred that is taking over your country. If this hatred does not cease, your evolution will be in danger. Know that we had hatred when we walked the earth during the time of Jesus. Today, I feel that the same hatred is present, and those of you that have been chosen to carry forth the messages of Jesus will face much of that same hatred. That hatred is very prevalent in your government and men in power; they are using that hatred to control the common people that live and worship in your country. Hopefully, those who understand and love our Lord will be able to take control and overcome the terrible obstacles that have been placed before your country. Not only do you have foreign countries that despise your freedom and love of God, you have individuals within that will tear your country apart for their own power. Hopefully those of you that understand this and have the ability to speak of the love of our Lord will have a lasting effect and will be able to overcome the obstacles that have been placed before you.

Know that those who love God and live good lives will be with him in his heaven. Those that speak against him and defy his existence will suffer his wrath and know the lower level of heaven. Those of us over here want you to understand that God is never to be feared; only those that create unforgivable sins should fear him. Even those that sin and are not forgiven are loved. They will have time to contemplate what they have done, and they will be able to, at some time, return to the lower realms, reincarnate, and make up for the evil they have done. As I said, tonight is a wonderful night! I only speak the words of love and faith that were spoken at the time Jesus walked the earth. Know the power of God! Know the power of love! And know the power of faith, and with that in your heart, you will certainly find the grace and love of our Lord in heaven. With that message, I will now answer some of your questions

Soul Life before Timothy

In previous chapters, we have discussed at length the fact that a soul has to serve God in many lifetimes before it is trusted to enter the highest level of heaven and be close to our Lord. I began by asking if he ever walked the earth before his lifetime as Timothy. His answer was this:

Yes; I walked the earth at the time of Moses as he led the people to the Holy Land. I was with him, and I assisted him in that lifetime.

When I asked Timothy if he ever served our Lord on other planets, he replied:

Yes; I served our Lord thousands of times on other planets. You humans are a very, very young culture. You have much to learn; we have been serving our Lord for millions of years in other worlds and other environments. Hopefully, with our help, you will learn enough to survive and prosper with the other intelligent cultures.

Once again, we see that survival of the human race is not an assured thing. We are continually being told that we have a lot to learn.

Early Life

I started inquiring about the early life of Timothy by asking him what year he was born. The answer was this:

I was born around 4 or 5 AD. As you know, our records were not very complete in those days.

"Where were you born?"

I was born in the same area of Judea near Nazareth.

It is assumed that his father was Greek and his mother Jewish. I asked him to describe his parents for us.

Yes; my father's name was Amos, and my mother's name was Esther. We were moderately wealthy Romans, and they were able to educate me.

"Did you have any brothers or sisters?"

Yes, I had two sisters and a brother.

"In what religion were you raised?"

I was raised in the Jewish faith.

That confirmed what I had read when researching Timothy. I asked how his mother was converted to Christianity.

My mother learned of Jesus as he lived and taught. There were times that she actually went to hear him speak. She was convinced of the one God, and my mother and father became true believers.

"Did your mother know or meet Jesus while he was on his ministries?"

Yes; she met him on several occasions and was very, very impressed. All she could speak of was how he showed the loving energy for everyone that was around him.

Connie and I can vouch for his loving energy when we are receiving his messages. Timothy's mother's experiences opened the door for Timothy to follow his karmic path. Next, I inquired if he had been taught to read and write.

Yes, my parents taught me to read and write. I was very privileged to have that ability.

It was a time when only the wealthy had the opportunity to be educated. Most of the individuals taught by Jesus were poor and uneducated.

Ministries of Saint Timothy

I asked him if he ever met Jesus in life. His reply was this:

> *No, I was never honored to have met our Lord. I was around those who spoke of him, and I was convinced that he was the Son of God.*

"Did you ever meet Mother Mary?"

> *No; I never met her until I came home to heaven. She was one of the souls that was waiting for me when I passed and came home.*

By the time Timothy began his ministries, Mary and Joseph would have been helping raise the family of Jesus. I inquired how Timothy was introduced to the belief in the one God.

> *As I said earlier, my parents were convinced of the one God, and they went out of their way to teach me the words that our Lord spoke.*

It is widely written that Timothy and Saint Paul were inseparable. My next question was, "How were you introduced to Paul?"

> *After the Resurrection of our Lord and when he appeared to Paul, Paul became one of his most fervent spokesmen. A friend of mine introduced me to Paul, and I could see that he emanated the same love of God that was shown by our Lord.*

"Can you describe Paul for us?"

> *As you all know, Paul was a Roman Pharisee and crucified Christians. Upon seeing our Lord after the Resurrection, he became an entirely different person. He did all he could to show love for those that he previously persecuted. Paul had a very strong personality. I was a little bit on the timid side, so we made a perfect pair. His outspoken traits more than made up for me being bashful around others.*

"In what year did you meet Paul?"

I met Paul about a year after the Resurrection.

In our interview with Paul, he mentioned that in the beginning there was some resistance from the other disciples because of his role in persecuting Christians before his conversion. I asked Timothy if he ever met any of the other disciples.

Yes, I was introduced to several of the other disciples. I met Peter; I met Matthew and several of the others. At first, they were a bit distrustful of us, because they knew of Paul's previous history with Christians.

"How old were you when you were introduced to Paul?"

I was around 26 or 27 years old.

"What was your occupation before you met Paul?"

I was trying to manage the affairs of my parents. As I said before, they were fairly wealthy and owned properties and farms, and I tried to watch over those properties for them.

"Why did you decide to leave the wealth and comfort of your family and become a disciple for Paul?"

Paul was so dynamic and spoke so highly of our Lord; his teachings were so overwhelming that I immediately decided to dedicate my life to spreading the words of our Lord.

Many of the followers were accompanied by their families. I inquired if Timothy was ever married.

No; I considered it, but upon meeting Paul, I decided that I would dedicate all my remaining time to speaking the words of our Lord.

The gospels describe Timothy as being of poor health during his lifetime. The patronage of the Catholic Church indicates that prayers should be directed to him in cases of stomach and intestinal disorders. My next question addressed whether he had any physical disorders during that lifetime. He replied:

Yes; I was always troubled with stomach problems. It seems as though whatever I ate would make me ill.

Not even the holiest of spirits are spared from human frailties. The gospels indicate that he and Paul traveled and worked together until Paul was martyred. I asked if he and Paul spent much time together during their ministries. The answer was this:

Yes; we were basically inseparable. He had so much knowledge about the words of our Lord! He had spent time with the other disciples before I met him, and he knew much. I was very impressed with his knowledge.

After years of spreading the words of Jesus, Paul was imprisoned and sentenced to death by the Romans. It is written that Timothy was allowed to visit and spend time with Paul in prison. I questioned whether he visited Paul in prison before he was martyred.

Yes; as he was awaiting the end of his life, I was allowed to come and visit him in prison. He gave me instructions for carrying on his teachings. He explained that if his words were to be to carried forward, I would have to be the one to speak them, and write them as well.

It is also written that Timothy was also put into prison by the Romans. When I asked if that was true, the reply was this:

Yes; I was imprisoned around the time that Paul was in prison. The Romans realized that if both of us were killed or left in jail, there would be an uprising among the young Christian community; for that reason, I was released from jail.

"What did you do after Paul was executed?"

I did my best to continue his teachings. Paul attempted to speak among the Jewish community; I attempted to follow in his footsteps.

Life after Paul

The execution of Paul must have been devastating to Timothy. He went on to establish churches and spread the word of the one God. I inquired where he preached the words of God. He replied:

I actually preached in many countries. The others were busy in the areas around Judea. I went to Greece, but it was very difficult there. I traveled to parts of Persia and what is now Egypt.

The gospels refer to his preaching and establishing churches in Macedonia. During this period of Roman rule, Macedonia was what is today northern and central Greece. He referred to how difficult it was to teach the words of God in Greece. I asked how he reacted to nonbelievers.

I treated them with patience, for I realized how radical the words of our Lord were for the times. The Romans had followed a pagan religion for many years. When I would run into a true nonbeliever, I would simply walk away. There was no reason for me to incur violence or to argue with them. Today you will find that there will be many that will refuse to believe that Barry and Connie speak the words of our Lord. You must try to convince them, but if they are inconvincible, it will do you no good to continue to attempt their conversion.

That is how we react to those that question our work. My next question inquired how he died.

I was actually stoned to death.

That corresponds to what is written in the gospels. "At what age were you stoned to death?"

I was around 50 years old. The Romans finally decided that I was a danger to them. They generated a mob of nonbelievers, and it was that mob that stoned me to death.

Greece being a difficult place to teach may have been an understatement. Many of the disciples and followers were martyred in Greece. I inquired what he considers his greatest contribution to spreading the words of God.

In life, I feel that I was quite successful in converting others to the one God. In heaven, I feel that I have been very helpful in guiding those that return to speak the words of our God. Many have been sent back. Many have been successful, but unfortunately many have failed. Hopefully we will have more success as our abilities to communicate with humans increase.

Unfortunately, the current high technical communication methods available seem to be leading individuals away from God.

Life after Death

Since incarnate lifetimes are a blink of the eye compared to your soul lifetime, much of the time, your soul is in heaven. I asked Timothy, "Who was present to meet you when you returned home to heaven?"

Jesus was waiting for me. Paul was there, and the soul of Moses as well. It was an incredible homecoming; it made all the pain I suffered at the end worthwhile.

I can only imagine what that must have been like. During the other interviews, I had been asking the holy spirits to describe heaven for us. Here is how Timothy answered the question:

As you have been told by the others, heaven is literally indescribable. The colors are very vivid; there is only love over here. There is no evil in the seven realms. Those that bring evil to this side have been sent to the lowest area. Evil is created after the soul returns to an incarnate life. Once again, heaven is the true home of your souls. Do not fear death! Death will be but the beginning of your homeward journey.

"What is your current role in heaven?"

I act as an adviser to those that are preparing to return and speak the words of our Lord. I helped prepare yours and Connie's life plan, so therefore I am very proud of what you are now accomplishing. There will be others that will be sent back. There will be those that will continue after you and Connie are no longer capable of doing this.

Timothy came through for us when we were beginning our education in board channeling several years ago. I can assure you that at that time, Connie and I had no idea of what the future was holding for us. Having helped with our life plans, he spent more time guiding us than I ever realized. I inquired what it was like to be close to Jesus in heaven.

To be close to Jesus is to feel the glow of love like you have never felt in your lifetime. Only in the presence of our Lord can you feel such a wholeness and inner love. He never speaks unkindly or in any type of a derogatory manner; he never shows any anger. He treats us all as members of his flock. There is really no way I can describe it; it is something that you have to see for yourself.

"Have you ever reincarnated since your life as Timothy?"

No; I have served our Lord on this side in many ways. I have attempted to guide others on Earth; in many instances, it was quite difficult. I am very happy that you have the ability to communicate my words! It is sometimes very frustrating to try to guide others and to be ignored.

"Will you ever reincarnate on Earth again?"

I will do what my Lord requests of me. If he feels that I should return, I will certainly accept that mission.

Since Connie and I are, at least for the current time, living an incarnate life, and especially since Timothy had just informed us he had helped with our life plan, I thought I would ask him why Connie and I were sent back for this lifetime.

When you are on this side, your souls are trusted companions and messengers of our Lord. You were sent back and given the gift to speak the words of our Lord and to pass on the truth of his messages and of his life. You were also given the ability to write. The books that you have written currently lay the foundation to what is to come. The most important aspect of your life will be the books concerning the life, messages and teachings of our Lord. This book you are completing will, in effect, be like a contemporary gospel, bringing individuals the messages of our Lord and the words of those of us that are close to the Christ and also speak for him.

The more we learn, the more amazed we are! It seems as though some souls are sent back, and others remain on the other side and act as guides. I inquired why some souls remain in heaven, while others, like Connie and I, are sent back to multiple incarnate lifetimes.

Certain souls have a history of serving our Lord. Many are trusted enough to be sent back. You and Connie are highly trusted, and we knew that by sending the two of you back together, you would both succeed in bringing others the words of his love.

I guess that defines a new meaning for *soulmates*.

Gospels and Words of Timothy

The two gospels of First and Second Timothy are believed to be epistles of instruction authored by Paul to Timothy. I asked Timothy if the written gospels accurately depict his life and ministries.

Somewhat; once again, there are instances where certain things in my life were exaggerated. Basically, the gospels that are written concerning me are relatively accurate.

"What are the greatest discrepancies between your gospel's contributions and what you actually wrote?"

I was told of reincarnation; the other disciples spoke of it, but I found it very difficult to understand. I did write about it, and I found out when I returned home that reincarnation was really the key to spiritual growth.

Reincarnation is a difficult concept for present-day individuals to understand. After all, the church has been preaching for 2,000 years that the soul only gets a single opportunity to get it right. I know from personal experience that whenever you speak against the written words of the Bible, you experience hatred. I asked the Saint to compare the hatred we see today with what he experienced in his lifetime as Timothy. He replied:

I think that we experienced more hatred 2,000 years ago than you do today. Remember that we were trying to change one of the most violent cultures of all time, from paganism to the belief in the one God. Today there is much hatred, and Satan is definitely growing, but if you follow the commands and the information you are given and do your best, Satan will definitely be defeated.

"What can we do to lessen the hatred we see today?"

You must show love to others; you must speak of love to others; you must be kind to others; you must live and treat others as you wish to be treated. If you do not speak and pass on evil, others will notice and hopefully follow your direction.

Very sound advice! Since we were conducting the interview on Facebook Live for our group, Words of God Then and Now, I asked Timothy if he had a message for members of the group.

Yes; we are very proud of those that have joined your group and gathered to listen and read the words of faith and love that have been given to them. It is our hope that those members will continue to bring others forward and teach them the truth and the true words of Jesus the Christ. You will be given much more information as time progresses. Use the time that you have to study and learn the words that have been given to you. Know that the words that are spoken to this group are the true and unaltered teachings of our Lord. Do not ever fear that God is not with you every moment of every day! Do not despair or be frustrated; remember that God always wins. There will be times of doubt and self-induced fear that you are alone. Do not listen to those feelings, just simply know that you will succeed, because God has willed that you will succeed.

It is always an asset to have God on your side. I inquired what we can do to better spread the words of our Lord.

Study what has been given to you. The more that you know and understand our messages, the more effective you will be in bringing others to God.

"What does Jesus want us to do to make this world better?"

Learn the truth of his words and speak them to others. Show his love to others and share his commitment to God, and you will have a better world.

Very timely and wise words. Our session with Saint Timothy the Apostle was coming to an end. I asked him if he had a final message for the listeners.

Yes; I am honored that I had the opportunity to speak with you this evening. It felt very good to once again be able to speak of the love of our Lord. I will return when necessary and help direct the members of your group and the ones that will join and also follow his teachings. Tonight has been a miraculous evening. I am so happy that I had this opportunity! I am honored that our Lord asked me to do this. From this day forward, know that his love is all-encompassing and will be with you and help to guide humans toward a better and happier existence with these words I left with you tonight. God bless you all, thank you for listening, and please join us in making this a more loving and happier world for all! Amen!

I thanked him for a very enlightening and inspirational channeling session.

CHAPTER 10

Saint Thomas

Who hasn't heard the term "doubting Thomas"? That phrase comes from the fact that Saint Thomas doubted the Resurrection of Jesus until our Lord appeared to him. There is minimal information about Saint Thomas in the Bible. Portions of his gospels have been discovered, but they are incomplete and often have contradictory comments. We are told that he was one of the disciples chosen to see Jesus after the Crucifixion, but we know little about his role as an apostle. It is written that Thomas traveled as far as India, where he was subsequently martyred. His remains are said to be held in the Church of Saint Thomas the Apostle in Ortona, Italy.

The Incredulity of Saint Thomas – Giovanni Bertucci cc1510 – National Gallery, London, UK.

Message of Saint Thomas

In July of 2018, the spirit of Saint Thomas blessed us by giving us a message and answering our questions in a Facebook Live session. Here is his message for all:

I want all of your listeners to know that I am watching over the people of your country and want to warn you that Satan is very active. Jesus wants all to spread the words of God and his love. If all of you do that, you will make a huge difference. God knows that you will do your best! Jesus, when he walked the earth, was met with distrust and malice. It was not easy for us to speak his words. After his Crucifixion, it became difficult for us to speak. The Romans made it very, very difficult. Many of us were martyred attempting to spread his words. Today it is different. You will face ridicule and nonbelievers. You will also face those that will refuse to understand that all the words in the Bible are not correct. Those individuals will make it difficult. God knows what you are up against. He will try to help, but free will will magnify the effect of Satan. Just be aware that all will be well, and your words will make a difference. Tonight, I want you to know that I will help and watch over you as well. There are many that are on my side that will support you; do not ever think that you are alone, God is always with you. Tonight is the first time I have been with Barry and Connie; they speak our words and those of God. Know that what they say is the truth. I will now answer your questions.

Once again, we heard the message that evil is increasing in the world and everyone should do their best to spread the words of God and slow the advance of evil.

Personal Life of Thomas

This was the first time we had been blessed to speak with the Saint, so out of respect, I asked how he would like us to refer to him. His reply was this:

Thomas is fine.

Thomas is one of the highest-ranking spirits in the soul family of Jesus. To have been assigned the important role of disciple 2,000 years ago, he must have had a long soul history with God, long before humans walked the earth. I asked him if he had ever reincarnated on other planets.

Of course; my life as Thomas is my only human life. I have lived thousands of times on other planets, where I spoke the teachings of God.

It is not easy for a soul to become a close servant of God. I inquired what his role was in the soul family of God before he returned as Thomas.

It is as I just said. I went wherever I was asked by God.

Once again, we see the overwhelming power of our God as he watches over our galaxy. I had read that it was believed that Thomas was related to Jesus. When I asked the question, the answer was this:

No, I was not related.

"Where were you born?"

Judea.

At that time, there were no public schools or buses to get one there. My next question inquired if he had the ability to read and write.

Somewhat; as I grew older, my skills increased.

"What was your occupation?"

I, like many of my brothers, was a fisherman.

"Were you raised Jewish?"

Yes; that was the predominant religion of Judea at the time.

We often forget that the followers of Jesus were young men and, in all probability, would have had families. Very little personal information about the followers of Jesus is included in the Bible. I asked if Thomas had ever married.

Yes; I had a wife and three children.

"What was your wife's name?"

Esther.

It is hard to understand the sacrifices the followers of Jesus would have endured. I asked Thomas if he had to leave his family to follow Jesus. His reply was this:

At times they came along on shorter trips, but most of the time I was alone.

"How did you meet Jesus?"

I was introduced by Matthew.

"Were you among the early apostles?"

I joined the group in the first year.

"How old were you when you met Jesus?"

I was 18.

"So you were very young?"

Yes.

The more I learn about the followers, the more I am amazed by how young they were. We do have to remember that it was a time when men left the home at age 15, women would be married at 13, and the average life expectancy was around 35. I asked him if he knew John the Baptist.

I met him a couple of times, but his path was different from that of Jesus.

"Were you baptized?"

Yes, John did baptize me.

John the Baptist played a large role in the beginning years of the ministry of Jesus.

Thomas as an Apostle

We learned earlier that the followers were assigned roles as the group traveled around Judea. I asked Thomas if he had a specific role as an apostle.

My role was to find areas where we could sleep and eat. It was quite difficult to find space for everyone. Sometimes we would have to just sleep under the stars. Food was always a problem.

Keep in mind that this was not always a small group of people. We were told earlier that at times there were as many as 45 followers. If some of them brought their families, there could have been as many as 100 individuals that required food and housing.

"Did Jesus ever speak to you of reincarnation?"

Yes, but he never spoke of it to the people. It was too difficult of a concept.

"Did Jesus ever speak to you of an alien presence?"

He spoke of his powers on other worlds, but we did not totally understand what he was talking about.

I imagine it would have been very difficult to understand the concept of life on other planets if you were born 2,000 years ago. There are many individuals alive today that cannot understand the concept.

I asked Thomas if Jesus ever told him he was married.

No; I only learned that after I returned home.

Most of the information about Thomas written in the Bible occurs after the death of Jesus. I inquired if he was present at the Last Supper on the Mount of Olives. He replied:

Yes; it was a sad time for all of us. He told us that he would be leaving. He knew exactly what was going to happen.

"What did Jesus tell you was going to happen to him?"

He said that his time on Earth was nearing an end and that we would have to spread his words.

"Were you there when he was taken away?"

Yes, I was there, but he told us not to resist.

We had been told earlier that the only disciple present at the Crucifixion was Mary Magdalene. I asked Thomas why he was not present at the death of Jesus.

I feared for my own life. I am ashamed that I did not have the strength of our Lord.

"Who told you the details of the Crucifixion?"

The two Marys; they were present.

That confirms what we had been told before about who was present at the Crucifixion. My guess is that it was part of the plan that the others did not attend. Their presence was required to speak the words of our Lord and carry his ministry into the future. Had they suffered a similar fate as Jesus, his ministry may have ended.

After the Resurrection

We are told that Mary Magdalene and Mother Mary discovered that the tomb was empty, and Mary Magdalene was the first to witness Jesus after the Resurrection. I asked Thomas who told him the details of the death of Jesus.

The two Marys. They were present.

"Did you doubt that Christ had risen from the dead as Mary Magdalene described it?"

Yes; my faith was weak, and I regret having doubt.

"Why did you doubt that Christ had risen from the dead?"

I knew that death was the end and never considered the fact that Jesus would rise from the dead.

At that time, it would have been a supreme act of faith to accept that Jesus had risen from the dead. Unfortunately, there are many people walking the earth today that still do not accept that fact. I asked Thomas if there were any other disciples or followers that shared his doubts that Jesus had risen from the dead.

Yes; there were several others, but most believed Mary when she told us she saw him.

In life, Jesus realized that he had to perform miracles to convince the nonbelievers. He also realized that he had to perform the miracle of the Resurrection and appearing to his followers so they would be forever convinced that he had divine powers, both in life and after death.

A Doubter No More

John 20:24–29 tells the biblical story of Jesus appearing to Thomas:

> *Now Thomas (also known as Didymus), one of the Twelve, was not with the disciples when Jesus came. So the other disciples told him, "We have seen the Lord!" But he said to them, "Unless I see the nail marks in his hands and put my finger where the nails were, and put my hand into his side, I will not believe." A week later his disciples were in the house again, and Thomas was with them. Though the doors were locked, Jesus came and stood among them and said, "Peace be with you!" Then he said to Thomas, "Put your finger here; see my hands. Reach out your hand and put it into my side. Stop doubting and believe." Thomas said to him, "My Lord and my God!" Then Jesus told him, "Because you have seen me, you have believed; blessed are those who have not seen and yet have believed." (NIV)*

Having read the biblical version, I asked Thomas what Jesus said to him when he appeared after the Resurrection. He replied:

> *He said that I should feel his wounds that prove it was really him. He also said that I should now tell others of the miracle that I observed.*

"What did you say to Jesus?"

> *I cried and asked him to remain with us and that we needed him. He then told me that he must remain in heaven but that his words would live forever.*

His words would indeed live forever! Unfortunately, many of his words were distorted through the years by those seeking power.

Ministries of Thomas

After being one of the chosen few to witness the Resurrection of Jesus, Thomas began to travel and spread the words of the miracle he had observed and the words of the one God. I asked if anyone accompanied him on his ministries. The reply was this:

I was assisted by some of my followers.

Just as Thomas was a follower of Jesus, he converted others to follow him as well. Jesus convinced others of his powers by performing miracles. I inquired of Thomas if he had the ability to perform miracles as well.

Yes; I had the ability to heal others, just the same as you have that ability.

"What were your primary teachings when you spread the word of God after the Crucifixion?"

I always spoke about seeing the miracle of his Resurrection and the undying love of God.

It is taught that Thomas verified the Assumption of Mary, mother of Jesus, into heaven upon her death. The Catechism of the Catholic Church describes the death of Mary as follows:

The Most Blessed Virgin Mary, when the course of her earthly life was completed, was taken up body and soul into the glory of heaven, where she already shares in the glory of her Son's Resurrection, anticipating the resurrection of all members of His Body (NIV)

I asked Thomas if he was present at the death of Mary. He replied:

No; I was on a mission, speaking the words of God.

"Did you witness the Assumption of Mary?"

No, but Mary passed a normal death. There was no Assumption.

"Where did you preach the words of God?"

I spoke in many areas. I traveled to India to try to convert those people to the one God.

"Why did you choose India?"

No one else went there, and I felt it was necessary to spread God's words as widely as possible.

It is written that Saint Thomas was martyred in India. There is a population of Christians along the western coast of India who claim their ancestors were converted by Saint Thomas. It is claimed that he built seven churches along the Malabar Coast and was killed by a spear while praying. The story of his death states that he was buried in Mylapore, but his remains were later transported to Ortona, Italy. I asked if he was martyred. The reply was this:

Yes; I was killed by a spear.

"Why were you martyred?"

The local priests were upset that I was speaking against their teachings.

"Who had you killed?"

The religious leaders of the area.

"How old were you when you were killed?"

Fifty-six.

His remains are said to be entombed in the Church of Saint Thomas the Apostle in Italy. I asked if the relics attributed to him are real.

Yes; my remains were moved several times, but they are now secured.

In this instance, the writings concerning Thomas are accurate, and his remains have a secure resting place.

"Who greeted you when you entered heaven?"

I was greeted by Jesus and several of the other disciples.

"Have you ever reincarnated since you walked the earth as Thomas?"

No; I find that I can be more effective from this side.

"What is your role in heaven?"

I assist Jesus in trying to spread his words, just as we are doing tonight. I work on other planets as well when I am needed.

"Do Connie and I know you when we are on the other side?"

Of course; you and Connie are one of us when on the other side.

I still find it hard to believe that we are with them on the other side, but Connie and I have been blessed to bring you these messages.

The Gospel of Thomas

The Gospel of Thomas was discovered in 1945 at Nag Hammadi in Egypt. It is a Coptic manuscript with 114 statements attributed to Jesus. Some of the statements contain information that contrasts with what is written in the Bible, and others are similar to the words found in Matthew, Mark, Luke, and John.

Another gospel, the Acts of Thomas, dates to the early third century and tells the story of his evangelistic trips to India. Anyone having an interest in these gospels can easily find their translations on the internet. I questioned Thomas about his gospels by stating that he continually stated the words of Jesus and asking if any of the words were ever written down as he spoke them. Thomas replied:

Some, but most of his words were written from memory.

"Who recorded the words in your gospels?"

After the Crucifixion, I started to try to make some notes.

I mentioned that in his gospel the words of Jesus are written in parables and asked if these parables really reflected his words.

No; he spoke in very simple terms so we all could understand.

"How accurate are the words of your gospels?"

Some are accurate; some are not.

"Did you write of reincarnation in your gospel?"

Yes; I wrote that the soul energy has everlasting life and that it would return for multiple lifetimes.

"Why were your gospels not chosen for the Bible?"

My gospel was not complete, and Constantine only selected complete gospels.

"Does the gospel of the Acts of Thomas reflect your words?"

No; that was written much after my death and does not reflect my words.

Once again, we see that quite often the information written in the gospels bears little resemblance to the real events that occurred and the words spoken by our Lord and his apostles.

Parting Comments of Thomas

Throughout our interview with Thomas, I was impressed with his energy and answers to our questions. This is truly a spirit dedicated to serving God. As we were ending the interview, I asked him what he considered the most important message for humans. He replied:

> *You must follow the words of God if humans are to evolve. Many cultures have chosen not to follow his words, and they have vanished. It is our hope that humans will be one of the successful species; without God, you will fail!*

He was echoing the words of Jesus and the other apostles, pointing out that the evolution of humans is dependent on their ability to follow the message of love for others that was spoken by Jesus when he walked the earth.

As we ended the session, I asked if he had any final words for the people that were listening to our broadcast. He said:

> *Go forth and speak the words of God. God will bless and keep all who follow his words. I want to thank everyone that has listened tonight. God bless and keep you all. Amen!*

Our session with Thomas was a true inspiration. It is obvious that he is a doubter no more!

CHAPTER 11

Saint Paul the Apostle

Saint Paul the Apostle never met Jesus in life but became one of his greatest proponents. We are told that Paul is one of the greatest examples of the forgiveness of sins by God. Jewish by birth and named Saul, he became a Pharisee and persecuted early Christians and followers of Jesus. He was on his way to persecute Christians when Jesus appeared to him. His story is an inspiration to all of us that have not exactly followed the teachings of God in the past. If forgiveness was given to Paul, there is hope for all of us. During a Facebook Live session in June 2018, we had the honor of interviewing Saint Paul the Apostle.

Message of Saint Paul

I started by asking if he had a message for the listeners.

> *I am here to tonight to tell all of you my love of God. I walked a different path in learning of his love. In my youth, I was a Pharisee and actually persecuted Christians. My life changed when Jesus came to me and changed my life for the better. Until I knew the love of God, my life was empty and without true direction. Jesus showed me that a sinner can be forgiven and serve God. Since learning of the love of God, I became an ardent follower and tried to tell as many as possible of his love and the existence of the one God. Through my writings, many have learned of his love and forgiveness. I am the true example that anyone can be forgiven and lead a life assured they will dwell in the upper realms of heaven. Tonight is a very special night. Once again, I can speak of God to*

all of you. It is your mission to go forth and speak his words as well. Much has happened all around you that indicates the growth of Satan. Without all of you taking strong actions in the name of God, human evolution is in doubt. Have faith that you can all make a huge difference, just as I made a difference. God is with you all and will not allow you to fail; all you need is the confidence in your abilities to convince others. I will now answer your questions.

Serving God on Other Planets

One thing that we have learned by speaking to the high-ranking holy spirits is that their souls have been serving God long before humans walked the earth. I started by asking Paul if he had lived any prior lives with the soul of Jesus before he walked the earth as Paul. He replied:

Yes; I was with him many times before humans walked the earth.

Soul energies have had to earn their place as members of the soul family of God through many lifetimes. My next question addressed if he was a follower of Jesus on other planets.

Yes, as much as I served him during his lifetime.

"Can you give us the name of some of the other planets on which you served Jesus?"

Yes, but you will not recognize any of them. I was a Tulin, but you have no comprehension of that planet.

"Will you describe what those prior lives were like on the other planets?"

Yes; I was a follower and taught his message of love on all planets.

I have written several books based on channeling an alien spirit named Mou. In his last lifetime, Mou lived on a planet named Robbe, located on the far spiral of the Milky Way. It was his spirit that told us about the galactic power of God. In an earlier session, I had asked Paul if he ever lived an incarnate life on Mou's planet. He answered:

Yes.

I was starting to understand just how small our galaxy can be. I figured it was a long shot, but I asked if his soul ever knew Mou. His answer caught me by surprise.

The name was changed, but the soul is one of us.

I was beginning to understand just how much planning went into Connie's and my life plan. I asked if my alien spirit Mou's soul lived during the time of Jesus and was one of his followers. Paul answered:

Yes.

"So all of the experiences that Connie and I are having were arranged before we came back for this lifetime?"

Yes; you are simply following the plan.

The more I learn, the more I realize just how much there is to learn. I assume that the soul energy of Paul has lived on all the advanced planets in our galaxy, a very impressive feat taking millions of years. It is not easy to obtain the right to attain the same realm in heaven as God.

Life of Paul

I decided to obtain some personal information from Paul's childhood, so I asked him the religion of his parents.

They were Jews and raised me in that faith.

"Can you tell me approximately the year you were born?"

After Christ. AD 6.

"Were you ever a member of the Roman army?"

No; I became a Pharisee, but the Roman army supported what I ordered.

"Were you actually responsible for the killing of Christians?"

Yes; I truly regret that I persecuted and killed early followers of our Lord.

Paul is proof that there is no limit to the forgiveness of God if you change your life and truly have his love in your heart. We have been told many times that you enter the incarnate world with a detailed life plan. I asked Paul if, when he entered that lifetime, killing of Christians was part of that life plan.

Yes; I was doing what I was sent to do so that I could be forgiven. Forgiveness was a major lesson to be taught by my life.

"How old were you when Jesus was crucified?"

Twenty-four.

"Were you aware of the Crucifixion of Jesus when it took place?"

Yes; the other Pharisees spoke of his Crucifixion. Many of them became aware that they had made a mistake and that Jesus was really the Son of God.

I think being aware they made a mistake is a bit of an understatement. We have been told in earlier sessions that the Pharisees that killed Jesus were sent to the lower level of heaven and are still there. I asked if he was near Jerusalem at the time of the Crucifixion.

No.

I am sure it was part of his life plan to be away from Jerusalem at the time of the Crucifixion so that he did not become involved. The more I learn about the workings of God, the more I understand there are no coincidences. The story of the conversion of Paul is told in Acts 9:

Meanwhile, Saul was still breathing out murderous threats against the Lord's disciples. He went to the high priest and asked him for letters to the synagogues in Damascus, so that if he found any there who belonged to the Way, whether men or women, he might take them as prisoners to Jerusalem. As he neared Damascus on his journey, suddenly a light from heaven flashed around him. He fell to the ground and heard a voice say to him, "Saul, Saul, why do you persecute me?"

"Who are you, Lord?" Saul asked.

"I am Jesus, whom you are persecuting," he replied. "Now get up and go into the city, and you will be told what you must do."

The men traveling with Saul stood there speechless; they heard the sound but did not see anyone. Saul got up from the ground, but when he opened his eyes he could see nothing. So they led him by the hand into Damascus. For three days he was blind, and did not eat or drink anything. (Acts 9:1–9, NIV)

Conversion of Paul

I asked Paul if he would tell us about his encounter with Jesus.

I was on the road to Damascus to arrest some followers of our Lord. He appeared to me as in life but was surrounded by light. I knew this was no ordinary event. He spoke to me, and I fell upon my knees in his presence. The energy of God was overwhelming, and he told me to repent my sins and they would be forgiven. He then told me to go forth and tell of the miracle that had taken place before me.

"By what name did he refer to you?"

He referred to me as Saul.

"Were you struck blind as stated in the Bible?"

No; I was overwhelmed but did not lose my vision.

"Can you tell us the words that he spoke to you?"

He called me by name and told me that in spite of what I had done, that God still loved me and had a plan for the rest of my life. He spoke that I should bring others to the one God.

"Did he tell you that he was the Son of God?"

No; that was not necessary, as I was beholding the miracle of God.

"How did you know that it was really Jesus that appeared to you?"

There was no doubt. I could see the wounds of the Crucifixion.

As you can see, there is some variation in what Paul tells us actually happened with what is written in Acts. I find Paul's words much more believable than the exaggerated words written in the gospels. The appearance of Jesus to Paul was truly one of the great miracles associated with the Resurrection. I asked Paul what he did immediately after the encounter with Jesus.

I went into Damascus and meditated for several days as my mission became more clear.

"Why did Jesus choose such a person that had been so cruel to Christians?"

He wanted to show that all can be forgiven if they change their lives and follow the words of God.

This story of forgiveness is one of the most important teachings by our Lord. The story of Paul is proof that you can be forgiven if you truly accept the love of God in your heart and live your life according to his teachings.

Life after Seeing Jesus

We have also been told that you cannot live a life contrary to the teachings of Jesus and expect forgiveness at the end of your life. I asked Paul if he was baptized after seeing Jesus.

Yes; I felt it was necessary to cleanse my soul of my past life.

"Did you preach that Jesus was the Jewish Messiah?"

Yes; since I was Jewish, I tried to speak to other Jews. They would not accept that he was the Messiah.

They still do not accept that the Messiah came to them 2,000 years ago. I inquired what Paul could tell us about his early teachings.

I started by telling of the miracle I beheld with my own eyes and that Jesus had truly risen from the grave.

That would have been pretty convincing testimony, especially coming from an ex-Pharisee. The other disciples and followers must have found it difficult to accept a person that had persecuted Christians into their group. I asked Paul how he was accepted by the original disciples.

At first, they doubted my faith, but as time went by, they saw the proof of my conversion.

"Having never known Jesus in life, where did you get the information on which to base your teachings to others?"

The other disciples told me stories of the preachings of Jesus. I included those stories with what I had seen with my own eyes.

"Who accompanied you on your earlier missions?"

I was assisted by several who I converted.

Words of Saint Paul

Much of the information in the Bible is attributed to the words of Saint Paul; one of these is the book of Acts. I asked if his words were the basis for the book of Acts.

My words are the basis for that gospel.

"Do your words appear in any other books of the Bible?"

Yes, Corinthians.

While some of the words in the Bible are accurate, one of the purposes of me writing this book is to provide accurate information about when Jesus and the apostles walked the earth. I asked Paul if any of his words had been altered from the truth. He replied:

Somewhat, but most are fairly accurate.

"What do you consider the greatest alteration?"

I was never negative about women. Corinthians makes statements about women having to remain silent. Those were not my words but were added later.

I had planned to ask him questions about his attitude toward women, but he beat me to it. "So, you are saying that you were not anti-women in your life?"

Correct; that was added by the church to assert their authority.

St. Paul in Prison – Rembrandt – 1627 – Staatsgalerie, Stuttgart, Germany.

The End of His Life on Earth

There is a lot of uncertainty about how Paul was martyred. It is generally agreed that Nero had him killed sometime after the great fire of Rome. I asked him how he died.

I was crucified.

"Was there anything unusual about your crucifixion?"

Yes; I was crucified upside down.

"How old were you when you were killed?"

Forty-five.

"Who had you killed?"

The Romans.

"Why were you killed?"

They resented that I no longer was a part of the ruling class, and my words were not acceptable to them.

"Who greeted you when your soul first got to heaven?"

Jesus was waiting for me, as well as Abraham. I knew I was home.

We are told repeatedly that the true home of your soul is in heaven and that your visit to Earth in incarnate form is but a blink of the eye in the life of your soul. Just imagine being greeted by Jesus and Abraham when you enter heaven!

Life after Death

I asked Paul what it was like to know Jesus.

It is to know pure love.

We have been told this many times before. I inquired if he had ever reincarnated since his life as Paul.

No; I have remained his faithful servant on this side.

"What is your role in heaven?"

I assist those that want to follow our Lord.

Throughout the writing of my books about Jesus and his apostles, I have been helped continually by Saint Augustine. When I write, I can feel his presence, and he has contributed a huge amount of information. He was born in the fourth century and advanced many of the writings of the saints, including the works of Paul. I asked if Paul would comment on the fact that Augustine advanced his writings.

Yes; he still works with me to assist those that want to learn, as you and Connie.

It is truly amazing how the holy spirits work together to attempt to influence humans. As we were nearing the end of our session, I thought I would have him comment on a current event. At the time I was writing this chapter, the United States was having an immigration crisis that was stirring a lot of emotions among the citizens of our country. I asked him his opinion on how the government should handle such a crisis.

They must show compassion while protecting your country. Your country is the closest to the teachings of God and must be protected at all costs. Without the United States, mankind will not have leadership, and evolution will be in doubt. Without your country, belief in the one God will perish.

I asked him if he had a message for Connie and myself.

Yes; you are doing God's work. It is up to each individual to believe and follow the messages sent through you and Connie.

"Do you have a message for humans that are currently walking the earth?"

Yes; know that God is with each and every one of you. His powers are without end.

We have been told these statements many times. Our earnest hope is that people will understand and believe these messages. We were ending the session, so I asked him if he had a final message for those people that would be listening to the video or reading his statements.

You are observing a miracle! We are bringing you the words of God. Jesus will now give you a message.

A Message From Jesus

Once again, we were blessed with a live message from our Lord.

I want all of you to know that I have heard your prayers and will do my best to lead the people back to God. That is why we are here tonight. With my guidance, you cannot fail. Good will win over evil. Tonight, I once again bless each and every one of you. I extend my love to all who accept me in their hearts. Go in peace, and know you are never alone. Amen!

As we learned, Saint Paul is unique among the messengers of the words of God. He is proof that forgiveness is available for all that have the love of God in their hearts and seek his blessings.

CHAPTER 12

Toba, the Wife of Jesus

Just imagine what it would have been like to have been married to Jesus! If you read my previous book, *Spirits Speak: Channeling the Life of Jesus*, you know that Jesus was happily married to a woman named Toba, and they gave birth to five children. If you did not read that book, you might be choking at the idea that our Lord was married. I would point out that the concept of Jesus being married is not addressed in the Bible. It is part of the missing segments of his life not addressed in the good book.

We had channeled with Toba, his wife, on other occasions and found her spirit to be loving and informative.

A Message from the Wife of Jesus

In January of 2019, her spirit agreed to come forward and give us a message, as well as answer questions. Here is her message:

> *Good evening, I want all of you to know how happy and pleased I am to have this opportunity to speak to you. As Barry has said, I was married to Jesus when he walked the earth. He and I lived a wonderful, normal life together. We were together for over seven years and during that time had five children. I know that there are many of you out there that doubt that Barry is truly speaking my words. Rest assured that he is; my husband, Jesus, is also here with us tonight. He has already talked to Barry and Connie before the show, and he is here to support me.*

I want you to know that even though you have never heard of me before, I have assisted my husband in blessing and watching out for all of you. You have been told before that there are members of this group that have walked the earth when I and my husband were there. Some of you have been sent back to help carry forward our words, and I assist in watching over those of you that have been assigned this important task. Tonight, I want to speak of the love of our God! He loves each and every one of you, and in your hearts, you must return that love. When my husband walked the earth, he taught of love; his message was very simple. He spoke that if you hold love for others in your heart and treat them as you want to be treated, then evil will be defeated. No one wants to have evil perpetrated upon them, so if love is in your heart, your way is clear.

Today there is much evil in the world, and you must all ban together in order to defeat it. When my husband and I walked the earth, there was much evil, but it was a different nature. My husband was dedicated to teaching others to follow the one God. Today many people say that they do follow God, but they do not love him in their hearts; for that they will pay when they return home and face my husband's judgment. Tonight, I want all of you to focus on loving God. I want you to hold your families close to you, I want you to be good to one another, and I want you to love one another. It is time when you must get past the hatred that you hear on your news broadcast and social media. We watch all this from over here; we hate to hear the evil that is being spoken to all of you. Simply remember that love is the most important thing in your life. If you love God, if you love me, if you love your neighbors, your family, and all that are with you, then that love will be returned. If you show hatred and anger, then that form of evil will be passed on to others. When I walked the earth, I loved my husband with all my heart, I loved my children, and I tried to love all those around me. As I said, it was an incredibly difficult time, and losing my husband like that was terrible. Today I want to bring you this message, and with those words, I am now ready to answer those questions that you have prepared for me.

As she spoke to us, we could feel her loving energy.

Her Life

Since there is no mention in the gospels that Jesus was married, it is obvious that there is no information concerning his wife and family. We began by asking why there was no mention in the Bible that Jesus had a wife and family. She responded:

We were afraid that if any of the disciples or followers were told that Jesus was married, the word would get out to the Romans and they would hunt us down and kill us, as they murdered my husband.

That is precisely what we were told in my earlier book. In those days, residents of the Roman Empire were basically pagan or Jewish. Connie inquired as to how Toba was raised.

My family was Jewish, and I was raised in that religion.

"What was the occupation of your father?"

My father had properties, and basically, owning those properties kept him busy.

"In what town were you raised?"

I was raised in a small town near Nazareth.

"Did you have any brothers or sisters?"

Yes, I had two brothers and one sister.

In those days, there were no online dating services. We know that it was preordained that her soul would meet Jesus and that she was sent back for this role, but we asked how she was introduced.

I was introduced to Jesus by my father. My father knew many people and had some wealth. Jesus was a fisherman at that time and was helping supply food for my family.

"How old were you when you met Jesus?"

I was 14 years old; remember that in those days, we married early.

This was a time of much shorter life spans. The average life span was 35 years, but the child mortality rate was extremely high. Nearly half of the children of Rome died before the age of 10. The upside of this statistic is that if you were fortunate enough to reach the age of 10, you had a very good chance to live into your 40s or 50s. Females were considered to be of marrying age from the time they reached puberty. Also keep in mind that families were mostly poor, and if the girl married and moved out of the household, it was one less mouth to feed. I inquired what the young girl thought when she first met Jesus.

Well, first I thought he was very handsome, and when he spoke, I just melted. I could tell that this man was very, very special from the start. I felt his love, and I returned his love.

Not much different from a young girl falling in love today! "Did you know who he was before you married him?"

No, I had no idea. I just thought he was a good man and would make a very good husband.

"What did your father think of Jesus?"

My father was very impressed with him; he was a very good fisherman and was kind to all.

Apparently, he made a big hit with his future in-laws.

Married Life of Jesus

I realize that the concept of Jesus being happily married and raising children takes a little time to get used to. Connie began to ask her questions about her married life. "How old was Jesus when you married him?"

He was around 20 years old.

"Did Mary and Joseph attend the wedding?"

Absolutely; he was very close to his family.

Little is written about Mary and Joseph. We know she was present at his birth and death, but very little else is known. I asked Toba about her relationship with her in-laws.

They were wonderful people. My father and I, and my mother, loved being with them. Mary had a wonderful personality, as did Joseph. Mary was very positive and was always laughing. She was an incredible person, and her influence was especially important with raising our children.

It is hard to imagine having the Blessed Mother and Joseph as family members. The next question addressed where they lived when they raised their family.

A small town near Nazareth.

"How long were you married?"

Sadly, we were only married for around seven years.

"How many children did you and Jesus have?"

We had five children.

"Can you name the children for us?"

Our firstborn was our only daughter, named Sarah; then there was Ezequiel and Joshua and Seth and Luke. Luke was the youngest of the children.

"Were the children raised Jewish?"

No; my husband always taught of the one God, so we raised our children understanding that there was only one God in our universe.

"What was Jesus like with the children?"

He was an incredible parent; he would play with them and hold them. He would love to just sit there and tell them stories. He would speak of life in heaven, and he would tell them that when their days on Earth were finished that their life journey would continue.

That was probably a very stupid question. How else would our Lord be with children?

"Can you describe your children?"

Sarah was our only daughter, and sadly she was never very healthy; she passed at around 20 of your years, it was a very sad event for me. Fortunately, my husband was on the other side at the time, and he made her transition quite easy. My oldest son's name was Ezequiel; he was always very energetic and a lot like my husband. Joshua was our middle child; he had a wonderful personality and was always laughing, a lot like his grandmother. Seth was the serious one; he always took things to heart, he was the worrier in the family. He was a wonderful child, and he grew up to raise a wonderful family of his own. Luke was the youngest of my children; I have a special place in my heart for you and Luke. Luke raised a wonderful family as well.

When he walked the earth, Jesus was referred to as the Son of God, even though he was God incarnate. This was done so that his message was not overcomplicated for his disciples and the people. The next question addressed whether any of his children ever knew he was God incarnate.

No; he never told anyone that. He said that his words would be heard forever and his words would have influence on many people to come, but he never told them that he was God.

"Did any of the children ever join his ministry?"

No, they never joined his ministry, because had they joined, we feared that the Romans would find out.

"Where did you and Jesus raise your family?"

We tried to move away from Nazareth so that our life, which was very simple, would not gain the attention of the Romans. Jesus knew what was ahead for him, and he knew that his family had to live in a more remote place to remain safe.

"Did he ever show anger when his children misbehaved?"

No; he was the most patient father.

"Did your children raise their families worshipping the one God?"

Yes; we tried to explain to all of them that their father was very special and that they should continue to follow what he had taught us. Sadly, he was not around for that long of time with the kids, but I tried to tell them.

"How did Jesus support his family?"

Jesus was basically a fisherman; he was also a wonderful carpenter. He was talented and could do anything that he put his mind to.

"Did you discuss that your marriage would be kept a secret?"

Yes; he told me that it was very important that nothing would happen to me or the children. For that reason, I would not even speak his name to the others.

In my book *Spirits Speak: Channeling the Life of Jesus*, I devote an entire chapter to the married life of Jesus.

Preparing to Change the World

As Jesus approached his 28th year, he knew what was ahead in his life. Imagine what must have gone through his head, being happily married with a young family. John the Baptist had been sent back to prepare Jesus for his ministry. Connie asked Toba if she knew John the Baptist.

Yes; John was a good friend of our family, and we spent much time together.

"What did John tell you about Jesus?"

He told us that Jesus was special, and he told us that he held the key to the words that would allow us to gain access to heaven after we passed.

"What else did John tell you about Jesus?"

He said that he was the Son of God. We did not fully realize what he meant, and sometimes we thought that he wasn't serious.

"Were you present when Jesus was baptized?"

Yes, I was there, as was Sarah and Ezequiel; they shared the experience.

"Did you understand the significance of his baptism?"

No; John said that it was especially important that he baptize my husband. I know that he agreed, but I never understood the true significance of it.

John did exactly what he was sent back to do. He baptized our Lord, and the rest is history. With both Toba and Jesus knowing what was ahead for him, the time to part must have been emotionally excruciating. Connie asked Toba the words Jesus told her when he left for his ministries.

He said that I would never see him again, that the Romans would kill him, that he needed to speak to the masses and tell them of the one God and the importance of love for one another; he said that there would be a time that I would be joining him in his heaven.

"So when he left on his ministries, did you ever get to see him again?"

No; sadly, when he left, it was the last time that I laid eyes on him until I joined him in heaven.

Throughout his ministries, we are told that Jesus performed 57 miracles, 37 of which are mentioned in the Bible. We inquired if Toba ever saw him perform a miracle.

Yes; he performed a miracle on me. Of course, it is not written in the Bible, because my presence is never noted in the Bible. There was a time that I passed out and was on the ground, and apparently, I was awfully close to dying. My husband performed a miracle and healed me; that was the first miracle that he ever performed.

It is only appropriate that he performed his first miracle on one of the people he loved most in life.

Life after His Death

After Jesus left for his ministries, Toba was left with the responsibility of raising the family and keeping their existence a secret. We asked if she moved a lot after he left for their security.

Yes; we tried to move farther away from Nazareth. He said that it was important that I did everything that I could so the Romans did not connect me with him.

"How did you support the family after he left for his ministries?"

My father helped support us; as I said earlier, he had properties. Without his support, it would have been very difficult.

"Did you have help raising the children after his death?"

Yes; Mary and Joseph were very important in helping me raise the children. They moved closer to us, so we would be several miles apart, and whenever I needed help, they were always there.

It is impossible to imagine what it would have been like to be a single mother and raise a family in those days. Our next question addressed what that was like.

It was terribly difficult. It was not like today; the only hope that you would have would be that your family would help you, otherwise you would have to do anything required to exist.

"Did you have to work to help support the family?"

No; luckily my father had sufficient funds, and I was not forced to work.

Jesus was away from home for around three years when the Romans killed him. There would have been no way of her knowing what had taken place. The next question addressed how she learned about the death of her husband.

After his death, he appeared to me, and that was how I knew . . . He told me that the Romans had killed him, and now he was on his way to take his place in heaven. He told me when I passed I would be with him again; he told me not to grieve, but that was impossible.

"How did he appear to you after the Resurrection?"

He appeared as he did in life; I could see the wounds on his body, but he was just as he had appeared when we got married. He was a very handsome man, and even though he had been tortured, he was still one of the most beautiful sights I have ever seen.

After his death, Mary and Joseph returned to be close to the family of Jesus. Connie asked if Mary told her the gruesome details of his death.

Yes, it was terrible; to hear her recount it was one of the most emotional moments of my life. Mary and Joseph were heartbroken, they just . . . There were no words to describe the grief that she felt with what the Romans had done.

"Did you ever meet any of the disciples or apostles in life?"

No; my husband was truly clear that we should not speak to any of the disciples or apostles. We always feared for the safety of the family.

The requirement for secrecy was absolute! He only confided in Peter during his ministry that he was married with a family. His secret has been kept for 2,000 years. Connie inquired how old Toba was when she passed.

I was 45 of your years when I went home.

She must have received an amazing welcome.

Soul of Toba in Heaven

When the soul of Toba arrived home in heaven, she had completed an important chapter in the life of Jesus. She let him learn what it was like to be happily married and the joy of having children. Once on the other side, it is up to the free will of the soul to decide if it is going to return to an incarnate life. Connie asked Toba if she had ever reincarnated since the lifetime with Jesus.

No; a single lifetime with my husband is the only time that I have walked the earth.

"Will you ever reincarnate again?"

I would if my husband requests it. In the event that he chooses to return, he will not return in the form of Jesus, but it is entirely possible that I will be asked to return with him at some future time.

That answer once again confirms that there will not be a second coming of Christ. If God decides to come back, it will be in another physical form. Connie inquired if Toba would describe heaven for us.

Heaven is the most wonderful place! It is literally indescribable. When you want to be somewhere, you just think it and you are there; if you want to be with your family, you think about them, and they are with you. There is no requirement for food, and there is no evil over here; it is truly a wonderful place.

Now that her soul is reunited with her husband in heaven, we inquired what her current role is while on the other side.

I assist my husband in any way that I can. I help watch over those of you that have been sent back. I try to influence others, and I attempt to guide others to speak of love and to have the love of God in your heart.

Definitely an admirable role! Her coming to us on that evening is the personification of a soul attempting to spread the words of God.

A Message for Humans

An advanced soul such as Toba certainly has a unique perspective as to the behavior of humans. Connie inquired what, now that she can watch from heaven, her message would be for humans. Here is her reply:

My message to humans is that you must have the love of God in your heart, you must have the love of others, you must share, and you must help others. By helping and loving others, others will help and love you. As you pass on love, love will be passed on. Humans have been struggling with free will since God created them. Free will is what creates evil, and humans must overcome their egos and the evil that their free will brings upon them. Doing good is how you rise in the realms of heaven. The upper realms are far more desirable than the lower realms, and you will be judged, and if you live a life of love and helping others, you will progress in the realms of heaven.

Toba and Jesus walked the earth at a very turbulent time. Cruelty, evil, and greed were everywhere. We asked if she thought there was more evil now or when they walked the earth.

When we walked the earth, there was certainly much evil. At this time, there is also much evil. I do not think it is any worse now than when we were there. The Romans that worshipped pagan gods would protect their gods at all costs, and what they put the early Christians through was terrible. We would watch what was taking place from this side and just . . . We would cry to see the pain and suffering that was caused. Today there are certainly times that pain and suffering is brought upon others. For instance, at the time of the Holocaust, evil was probably as great as any time man has walked the earth. Today there is certainly much evil, but it is different. We are seeing much evil in your politicians, and they have the ability to destroy your country. It is time that love becomes the most important thing, in politics and your everyday lives.

"Did you ever live any other lifetimes with our Lord before you walked the earth as Toba?"

Of course; you humans have only been there for roughly 250,000 years. The soul energies of God have been around since the beginning. I have lived with the energy of Jesus on many other planets at many other times. We had led other cultures to learn of the one God and to live in peace. Living in peace is the lesson that the humans still have to learn.

I guess if they can succeed on other planets, they can succeed on earth. That is, assuming their patience does not run out. We asked the wife of Jesus if she had a final message for our listeners.

I want to thank all of you for listening tonight. I want you to know that Barry and Connie's words are our words. We are able to speak through Barry; when you hear his words, they are our words. When he says that he speaks the words of Jesus, he truly does speak for him. There will be a time that it will become more evident that

Barry and Connie have been sent back for this special mission. When that time comes, I hope that all of you will contribute in passing on our messages. Tonight has been a special treat; there is probably nothing more controversial than the fact that I was married to Jesus and that we lived a relatively normal life. Tonight, Jesus is here with me. He and I bless all of you. God bless all of you, and until we speak to you again, good night!

Her final message was certainly a vote of confidence for Connie and me. Hopefully, we can live up to the expectations of the holiest of spirits.

CHAPTER 13

Mary, Mother of Jesus

Throughout time, no individual, with the exception of Jesus, has been more idolized than Mary, the mother of Jesus. It is a basic tenet of the Christian doctrine that Mary was a virgin at the time of the birth of Jesus. The Catholic Church believes in the concept of the Immaculate Conception, in that she lived a life without sin and her body was assumed into heaven. Anyone that has prayed the Rosary has sung her praises. She has performed miracles at such places as Fatima. We have been blessed with her appearance on multiple occasions, and her spirit energy is impossible to explain. In this chapter, we will bring you the actual words of Mary as she brings us a message and speaks of her life.

Message of the Blessed Mother

In April of 2018, we were blessed with her presence during a Facebook Live session. Here is her story:

> *I want to tell all of you how much I love and watch over you. Together you will make a huge difference in speaking the words of my son. He is also here with us tonight and wants you to know that he also loves and watches over you. Tonight is a special evening. You all know that Barry and Connie speak his words and will continue to do so. It is very important that all of you speak his words as well. Words of God will defeat Satan. I want you all to go forth tonight with the knowledge that you will make a difference. You have been sent back to continue my son's mission on Earth. Many of you knew him when he walked the earth. Many of you*

were his faithful followers and apostles. God has arranged for you to be here tonight and will continue to bring you his words. I am here to help carry out your mission. My son knows all of you and will continue his blessings and love. Do not fear that you will fail; that is not possible with God's blessing. Know that Satan will fail! God has created the United States as the country most close to his teachings; many are trying to remove God from your country. You have been sent back to stop this from happening. Your politicians are forsaking you with their greed. From this time forward, know that things must change, or your country will lose God's blessings. Without those blessings, your country will fail. It is not too late; remember that God always wins. You are on the side of God, and you will win as well. I bless each and every one of you! My love for you is undying, and forever, from this day forward, you will have this special blessing and feel my loving energy. God bless all of you! Amen!

Much of the message was directed toward the members of our Facebook group, Words of God Then and Now. It was truly a message of love and direction on how we should be living our lives. I asked her if she had any other message for the listeners. She replied:

Jesus hears every word of prayer and will bless those that have love for him in their hearts; without that love, their lives will have a vast emptiness. The Holy Spirit will light your way; have no doubts when I tell you this.

Truly an inspiring message!

Believing the Unbelievable

I am fully aware that the vast majority of people that watched our session with Mary were saying there was no way this could actually be happening. Why would one of the most holy of spirits take her time to bring a message to the people over Facebook Live? I can assure you that when we are blessed with her presence, you can feel her loving energy as she gives us her message and answers our questions, but that will do little to convince the doubters. I began by asking if there was any way she could show the nonbelievers that she was really with us. She answered:

Those that refuse to believe will not know my love. There will be a time when I will prove to all the reality of my presence with you; until that time, you must have faith that I am here.

Connie and I will look forward to that moment, but we have total faith that we really are conversing with the Blessed Mother. No holy figure, with the exception of God, has more prayers directed to them than Mary. I inquired what it was like to have so many people directing their prayers to her.

Jesus is also hearing those prayers. I will watch over all who pray to me.

The Immaculate Conception – Bartolome Esteban Murillo – 1678 – Museo Nacional de Prado – Madrid, Spain.

"Do you have a special dedication to mothers who pray to you?"

Yes; I am watching over all mothers that are suffering and in need.

I asked her if it would be possible to describe what heaven is really like.

Heaven is the most wonderful place. We watch over individuals and try to guide them. It is a place where love is everywhere, and that is the guiding light.

We are continually told by spirits on the other side that heaven is indescribable and far exceeds anyone's expectations. I asked her if she would tell the listeners the true meaning of everlasting life.

Yes; your soul returns in many different lifetimes to learn and become close to God.

Once again, it is confirmed that when Jesus taught of everlasting life, he was speaking of reincarnation and the journey of the soul through multiple lifetimes. In my earlier chapter, I discussed the holy soul family of God and how members of it had lived multiple lifetimes on other planets in the service of God to have obtained the highest realm of heaven. I asked Mary if, before she walked the earth with Jesus, there was ever a time that their souls were together in prior lives. She answered:

Yes; we were on other planets, teaching love and cooperation, many times before.

"When you were on other planets with the spirit of Jesus, were you always his mother?"

No; we had many different relationships in those prior lifetimes.

As we noted before, there are many souls that have served God through many lifetimes. Just as humans have soul families, there is a soul family of God that serves him when called. I asked Mary if she would tell us about the soul family of God.

Yes; there are many souls that have served God throughout the millions of years by serving him on many planets, many times. Those souls still serve him when on the other side. When asked, these souls return to lifetimes and attempt to serve his will. One example of a soul that returned and was very successful is Billy Graham. The Reverend Graham was actually a reincarnated child of my son! He was sent back to spread the words of the love of God and did a wonderful job. He is now with us back on this side and is helping us from here.

"What is the best way to have people love each other and to make world peace?"

All must speak of God and have his love in their hearts. Unfortunately, that is a difficult task. Each of you can help, but it will take many more to get involved. That is why you must spread these words.

She just gave us some good information and a path for all to follow.

Life of Mary

Little is actually recorded about the life of Mary and Joseph. Little about Joseph is mentioned in either the scriptures or other gospels. One rendition even has Joseph at the age of 93 when Mary gives birth to Jesus. The last reference to Joseph in the Bible occurs in the story about Jesus as a 12-year-old in the temple. I asked Mary if she would describe the personality of her husband, Joseph. She replied:

> *Yes; he was a wonderful individual. He is still with me over here and serves our Lord on this side.*

The Bible states that Joseph was a carpenter. I asked Mary his occupation.

> *He was a carpenter, and a good one.*

The Bible indicates that Mary and Joseph were not married at the time of the birth of Jesus and she was a virgin at the time of the birth. I inquired if they were married and for how long at the time Jesus was born.

> *We were married for several years before giving birth to Jesus.*

Since they were married for several years, I asked if Jesus was their firstborn child. Her answer was this:

> *Yes, he was my firstborn.*

"How old were you when you gave birth to Jesus?"

> *Thirty-three.*

"How old was Joseph when Jesus was born?"

> *Forty-three.*

So much for the story that he was a very old man at the time of the birth of Jesus. I inquired when she knew Jesus was special.

I knew from the time Gabriel told me I was with child.

My guess is that having the angel Gabriel appear to you would make quite an impression, especially 2,000 years ago.

"How many children did you and Joseph have besides Jesus?"

Two.

"What were the names of his brother and sister?"

Sarah was the name of his sister, and Joshua was the name of his brother.

When Jesus married and had children, he named his daughter Sarah and one of his sons Joshua as well. My next question addressed what his brothers and sisters did with their lives. Her answer was this:

They led normal lives. Sarah married and had three children. Joshua also married and had two children; he worked as a carpenter, like his father.

"Did the brother and sister of Jesus follow his teachings?"

To some extent, but when my son started his mission, they never saw him again.

His brother and sister may have never learned how special Jesus really was.

Birth of Jesus

One of the best-documented events in the Bible is the birth of our Lord. I figured this would be a great opportunity to separate truth from fiction. I began by trying to clarify the time of year the birth took place.

Adoration of the Maji – Hendrick ter Brugghen – 1619 – Rijksmuseum, Amsterdam, Netherlands.

I believe it would correspond to what you call September.

The gospels tell us there was a steady stream of individuals that were led to view the baby Jesus, including shepherds and wise men. I asked if she and Joseph were surprised by all the attention that was directed toward him.

Yes; we did not expect that there would be so much attention for the newborn child.

My guess is the biggest surprise would have been the arrival of the entourage of the wise men. I inquired what Mary and Joseph thought when the wise men showed up to see the baby.

We were shocked; there were many in their group. When they gave us the presents, we did not know what to say. We were not used to being in the presence of such royalty.

"Did they tell you about their orders from King Herod?"

Yes; they said they were to report back to him and give Herod our location. They also told us that they would not do what Herod requested and they would leave by another route.

"How old was Jesus when they arrived?"

Around three months of age.

We had been told that before. There would have been no way for them to have known on their own that King Herod wanted to kill the baby. I inquired how she and Joseph found out that the life of Jesus was being threatened.

We suspected from what the wise men told us, but then the angel Gabriel also appeared and told us as well.

"How long did you remain in Bethlehem?"

We left immediately. The wise men left, and we left about the same time.

" How did you know where to go to protect the baby?"

We were receiving messages from Gabriel; he guided us and told us where to go.

It must have been very intimidating for the couple, knowing they had to flee to a foreign country in such dangerous times. "When you fled to Egypt, did you know anyone there?

No; we were strangers, but there was always divine help for us.

My feeling is that there is always divine help if you ask for it.

Raising Jesus

I inquired what Jesus was like as a child.

He lived a very normal childhood, much like any other child.

"Were you aware what was in store for Jesus?"

I knew he would spread the words of the one God.

In my previous book, *Spirits Speak: Channeling the Life of Jesus*, we devoted a chapter to the married life of our Lord. We told that Jesus was married for seven years to his wife, Toba, and they had five children: Sara, Ezequiel, Joshua, Seth, and Luke. I asked Mary if when Jesus and Toba were married, she and Joseph knew the family. She replied:

Yes; we helped with the children.

"Did you know Luke as a child?"

Yes; you were a good child and listened to your mother and me.

An interesting piece of information. Mary and Joseph are thought to have been Jewish. I inquired if she would explain the religious teachings she taught as they raised Jesus.

We taught of a single God; we knew Jesus was special and was sent to us by that one God.

After the death of King Herod the Great, Judea was ruled by his son, Herod Archelaus. A cruel and despotic ruler, he was removed from power by the Romans in AD 6 and exiled. It would not have been safe for the family of Jesus to have returned during that time. I inquired how they knew when it was safe to return to Judea.

Once again, Gabriel came to us and let us know that it was safe to return. We also heard that Herod had died and that his son was going to lose power.

"During the time your family was in Egypt, was Jesus ever in danger?"

No, we were always protected.

After returning to Judea, they moved farther north, to the vicinity of Nazareth. We were told earlier that at the age of 15, Jesus left home to begin his travels so he could observe the human suffering of man during this period. I asked Mary what she thought when the teenager left for his travels.

I was very worried, because it was a dangerous time, but once again Gabriel assured us that nothing would happen.

Gabriel was truly a guardian angel for the family.
Ministries of Jesus
I asked Mary her opinion of Toba, the wife of Jesus.

She was a wonderful and loving person. She would spare nothing to help raise the children.

"Did you live in the same town as Jesus when he was married?"

We did not live in the same town, but we were relatively close, so we could visit his family.

Not much different from today; grandparents want to stay close to visit their grandchildren. We were told that John the Baptist was very friendly with the family of Jesus. I asked Mary if she was friendly with him as well. She replied:

Yes; John was a friend of the family. He was very close to Jesus and his wife.

"What did you think when Jesus left for his ministries?

I knew that was his life plan, and he warned us that the Romans would kill him. I was very sad when he left, because I knew it was the beginning of the end.

There is no doubt these were strong individuals. Imagine knowing with certainty the future and that the end of the life of Jesus was rapidly approaching. I inquired if she ever traveled with him while he was on his ministries. She answered:

Sometimes; I did travel with him at the end.

Imagine what it would have been like to know that your son was at the end of his life plan.

Death of Jesus

As the time approached for the life of Jesus to end, he gathered his disciples and followers around him on the Mount of Olives and gave them the final blessing, knowing he was about to be arrested by the Romans. I asked Mary if she was with him on that final evening.

Pieta – Michelangelo – 1499 – St. Peter's Basilica, Vatican City.

Yes, I was there when he issued his final lesson to all the others. I was in tears, because I knew the end was near.

After he was taken by the Romans and the Pharisees, Jesus was brought to Pontius Pilate for trial. The procurator attempted to appease the Pharisees by having Jesus flogged, but to no avail. I inquired if Mary watched the trials.

From a distance.

It must have been heartbreaking to have witnessed the events that were taking place. The trials of Jesus were followed by the procession to Mt. Golgotha and the Crucifixion of our Lord. We have been told before that the only disciples to witness the Crucifixion were his mother Mary and Mary Magdalene, because the others feared they would be killed as well. I asked Mary why she decided to attend the death of her son.

The other disciples told me that they feared for their lives if they attended the Crucifixion. I did not want my son to die alone.

"Why did Jesus have to be crucified?"

He needed to be crucified so that others would always remember him. He feared that just the strength of his teaching would not be enough; such a brutal death would unite individuals around him.

There is no doubt that the brutal death of our Lord was remembered and changed the world. Mary Magdalene was the only disciple that attended the Crucifixion. I asked the mother of Jesus her opinion of Mary Magdalene.

Mary was also a very trusted disciple and very close to my son. Mary contributed greatly to the success of spreading his words of love. She accompanied me to the Crucifixion; it was also very difficult for her.

"Did you know Jesus was going to resurrect?"

He told us that he would have everlasting life and return. I did not fully realize what that meant.

It would have been very difficult for anyone to have realized the true extent of his words.

Life after Jesus

It is impossible to imagine the emotions and grief created when you watch your own son being martyred in the cruelest fashion possible before your eyes. I asked her what she could tell us about her life after the death of Jesus.

It was very difficult. I missed him very much, but I knew he was at the end of his life plan.

"Did you know that the Romans were going to kill him?"

Yes; he warned us, but it was a terrible time.

"Did Jesus give you instructions on what to do after his death?"

Yes; he told Joseph and me to help raise his family. When Jesus left home, you were only one year old, and he knew that it would take help to raise a family. He told us to keep the presence of his family a secret. He feared the Romans would retaliate and kill his family.

"What did you and Joseph do after the death of your son?"

We returned to Galilee and helped raise the children.

Luke, the youngest child, would have been four or five when Jesus was killed, and it would have been difficult for a single mother to raise five young children. As I wrote in my earlier book, Toba's father provided financial support to help raise the children, but it must have been an incredibly difficult time.

"Did Jesus ever appear to you after the Resurrection?"

No; he did appear to others, and they told me of his presence. It was more important that he appeared to the disciples than it was for him to appear to me. They needed to know that he had risen and that his life was indeed eternal.

"How did you deal with the aftermath of the Crucifixion?"

It was a terrible time for me and all that knew him. Until he rose from the grave, the disciples and those close to him spent their entire time in tears and in fear that he would never return. After I heard of his Resurrection, I felt better but still missed him terribly.

"Did you keep in contact with any of the disciples after the Crucifixion?"

Once I left them to return to the family, I only saw a few of them for short periods of time. Once again, secrecy was vital to protect the family.

We had been told earlier that Peter was the only disciple aware that Jesus was married. There was a good reason why the truth of the life of Jesus and his family was kept a secret, so much so that there is no mention of his married life in the gospels.

Opinions of Mary

During our sessions with Mary, I asked for her opinions on multiple subjects. Since the Catholic Church has elevated her to such a high status, I asked her for her opinion of the current church. She replied:

It has lost its true direction. The words of my son have been changed to strengthen the power of the church.

That answer will probably upset a lot of people. Next, I inquired her opinion about the virgin birth and Immaculate Conception.

That was added after the death of my son.

"What is your opinion of praying the Rosary?"

It is a guide for prayer, but just a guide. In prayer, you should have a conversation with God.

"What do you consider the greatest distortion of information concerning your life?"

The story of the Immaculate Conception. I lived a normal life. There were times that I sinned but was forgiven, as all of you can be forgiven.

It is amazing how the early writings were distorted to make the biblical characters godlike as conceived by the early monks. I asked her opinion of the current human race.

I am saddened by the growth of Satan, but I am excited about the possibility of defeating him once and for all. My son's words of love are capable of reaching many and hopefully having a lasting impact on mankind. Once the truth of the life of my son is known, many can move forward and spread his words of love.

"What would you tell us about trying to reconcile the information in the Bible with what is being taught here?"

The information in the Bible provides an overview of information about God and my son's life on Earth. Many of the details have been exaggerated by individuals attempting to gain power. Just remember that the basic teachings are correct, but the problems lie in the details. You will learn the truth here.

"Can you define the Holy Spirit?"

The Holy Spirit is the all-powerful and everlasting energy of God. It is a very difficult concept to understand how God can be present at all places. But his spirit is truly everywhere and all powerful.

"What is the role of the Holy Spirit?"

The role of the Holy Spirit is to watch over other incarnate souls and to offer guidance in their lives. Hopefully that guidance will affect their free will and they decide not to live a life of evil.

At the time we conducted this session with Mary, another act of evil in the form of a mass shooting had killed members of the Jewish faith in Pittsburg, Pennsylvania. I asked her, "What is the lesson being learned from this event?"

This was an example of the power of Satan to overcome others and have them perform his will. This was an act of absolute and terrible hatred. All should look at this as an example of what Satan is capable of and understand he needs to be defeated.

Unfortunately, humans can be very slow learners. We have seen in the past how evil can grow and result in the deaths of millions of people, in spite of the attempts by the spirits on the other side to stop it. I asked Mary what her message would be for the future of humans.

Love God, and all will be well. If you fail to have the love of God in your hearts, you will fail.

We can only hope that individuals will pay attention to her words. People are continuously praying to her to perform miracles. I asked Mary what she considered her greatest miracle. Her answer was this:

Fatima.

For those of you not familiar with the miracle of Fatima, Mary appeared to three shepherd children and prophesized that she would appear and perform a miracle. The chosen date was October 13, 1917, and the event took place in Fatima, Portugal. A large crowd gathered, and it is said that for a 10-minute period, the sun appeared to zigzag in the sky and emit multicolored light. I asked her what she could tell us about the miracle.

I came to the children, and they spoke of my presence.

"One description claimed there were three days of darkness."

That did not happen.

"What was the third miracle of Fatima?"

There was no third miracle.

So much for that rumor. She told us in previous sessions that there would be a time that she would prove the reality of her presence with us, or in other words, perform a miracle to show we were really in her presence. I inquired of this, and she answered:

That time will take place after the book describing the life of my son is published. At that time, there will be absolutely no doubt that you are speaking his words and mine as well.

While I am aware of the miracle of her presence, I can only hope she will prove it to all.

More Messages of Mary

In November of 2018, we were once again blessed with the spirit presence of the Blessed Mother when we channeled her during a Facebook Live session. Here is her message from that event:

I am pleased to once again have the opportunity to speak with all the wonderful members of this group. I want all of you to know that my son and I watch over you, love you, and appreciate all that you are doing to help spread the words of love that my son spoke when he walked the earth. Tonight, I want you to know that much depends upon your abilities to fulfill the missions that you were sent back for. Satan is growing; that is irrefutable! What each and every one of you must do is spread the words of love that were spoken by my son and have been given to you by Connie and Barry. The words that you hear in this place are the actual words of me and of my son. Have no doubts; there will be many that try to disprove the truth of what we speak. They will have to face that judgment at a later time, when they come home. For the present time, just know that all of you are special in the eyes of me and my son.

When Jesus walked the earth, it was also a difficult time. Modern atheists and secularists are trying to take the love of God from the people. You cannot let that happen! Without having God in your heart, evolution will be fruitless. Know that we will do all we can to assist you. Hopefully, the free will of evil will not win out. We have sent Barry and Connie back to begin this important movement. When the book comes out about the life of my son, you will all have the information that will be required for you to go forth and speak the words. Until that time, pay attention to the messages that you receive here. All can benefit from the true knowledge of what took place when my son walked the earth. Tonight, as I said, is very special. When I am finished answering questions, my son will have a message for you as well. Know that we watch over you! Never doubt that fact; there are times that you will feel depressed and down because you think your messages are not being heard. Never doubt that you will be successful. God always wins, and with that, I will answer questions for you.

Whenever we are channeling with the Blessed Mother, we can feel her loving energy. I asked her if there was any way she could have the listeners feel her energy so they could better understand the miracle of her presence. She replied:

I am trying to let all feel the energy of my love. In the future, there will be times that each will feel that energy independently, but for now just know that my energy is with each and every one of you.

On that November evening, I asked Mother Mary if she had a final message.

Yes; just understand that God is with you and always will be with you! When your journey in this lifetime ends, you will go home, and you will be with my son and me in heaven. If you choose to follow evil, you will not be with us but will be in a lower realm in heaven. You are responsible for your own free will and ego. You must control that and spread words of love! Spread the word of the love of God. It is that simple! I will return and help you in the future; my love for each of you is never-ending. Amen!

As we approached the Christmas season in 2018, we were blessed with a special message from Mary as we prepared for the celebration of the birth of her son. Here is her message:

God bless all of you here tonight, for this is that time we gather together to honor the entrance of my son into this world. He came forward to bring the good word of God to all. Thousands of years ago, my son was born. It was a special time for Joseph and me, but it also was a time of wonder for the world. We were not prepared for all of those who came to worship my son as a baby. We were astonished that simple individuals such as shepherds showed up to view my son; we were astonished when the wise men came forward to visit us. They were a huge group of men and royalty. We had never seen anything like it. They brought us gifts of frankincense and myrrh, as written in the gospels. They told us they had the gift to prophesy that the Messiah would be born, and they came forth to visit with him. They also warned us that Herod had planned to kill the baby and that we were to use the presents that they gave us to pay for the journey of our family to safety.

On that simple day, all of the future of mankind changed forever. God came to Earth in the form of my son Jesus. He was a wonderful child; he lived and he loved and at the appropriate time began a ministry that was to change the world. At the time of his birth, as a young mother, I felt nothing but joy. When I looked into his eyes, I knew that he was special. Even as the youngest infant, he showed love, and that love would follow him throughout his life. I want to thank all of you for listening here tonight. Please go forth and spend the time that you have with your family; know that the moments with your family members are precious. Do not waste them by fighting and showing hatred toward them; let the love that my son showed for the world be reflected in each and every one of your hearts. Let that love come forth and lead the way for others to show it as well. Let there be no hatred at this wonderful celebration season! Do not become over commercialized; let the day of celebration be one of meditation and family togetherness. This is a period of joy unto the world. Do what you can to spread that joy and love, and with those words, I will leave you tonight. Know that I bless you and watch over you. With these words, I will say, God bless each and every one of you, and good night.

Just as the Blessed Mother gave us a special message for Christmas, she came to us on Good Friday 2019 and gave us her special insight into the Crucifixion and Resurrection. Here is that special message:

Good evening! Tonight, I want to tell you just how much I love every one of you. Tonight is a very bittersweet time for me. This is the time that I remember and think about the most horrific day of my life when I walked the earth as the mother of Jesus. I cannot tell you the grief that I felt, the tears that I shed, and the horrible feeling knowing that my blessed son would no longer walk the earth. He was a true inspiration for all in his life. His words moved millions and are still spoken today. On that terrible day, I and Mary Magdalene were the only two that were present to watch his passing. I cannot tell you how much it means to me to be able to share with you my memories of that horrific day.

My son passed with great dignity. The soldiers that were present, many of them who knew that my son was special felt the same emotion that I felt at his passing. They were simply doing and following the orders of the Pharisees. Upon his death we placed his body in the tomb that was owned by Joseph of Arimathea. We felt sad that we were not allowed to prepare his body for burial, but the Romans sealed the tomb for fear that his followers would remove his body from the tomb. Mary and I returned to the tomb several days later in order to beg the Romans to allow us to prepare my son's body for burial. When we arrived, the tomb was empty, and we thought for sure that somebody had stolen the body of my son! It only added to the terrible grief that we were still feeling.

The other disciples had not attended the Crucifixion, for fear that they would be involved and meet the same fate as my son. All that you have learned of the death of my son has been told to others by Mary and myself. The fact that the tomb was empty only added to our horrendous grief. We had no idea that what had taken place was the greatest miracle that ever happened on your planet Earth! We did not know at the time that my son had resurrected from the grave. He had told us in life that he would return to us, but we never fully understood what he was referring to. The miracle of the Resurrection is the miracle and proof of our God and his love for humans! Without the Resurrection, none would know the true fact that my son was God incarnate. Today, you commemorate the day that allowed for the Resurrection! The loss of my son was an incredible tragedy for the lives of Joseph, myself, and all his followers and disciples. The fact that he resurrected and showed himself to his disciples and followers is proof of the ultimate power of our God! Know that God is with you, loves you, and watches over each and every one of you. It is a time where all must speak of his love and try to stop the growth of evil energy that is thriving in your country today. Today, as I said, is a day of commemoration and mourning the death of my son. On Sunday, you will celebrate the fact that he rose from the grave and took his place as God in heaven so that he can continue to guide and watch over all. Tonight, I want you to know that I love and bless each one of you that will hear this. With those words, I am going to let my son bring you his message.

The Blessed Mother Mary still watches over and brings us messages of love and truth. Her words in this chapter are a blessing for all of us.

CHAPTER 14

Messages of Jesus

Jesus has blessed us by allowing Connie and me to channel his messages in live events on the internet. Many of these sessions can be seen on my YouTube channel. Some of you will doubt that I am capable of speaking his words. Approach this chapter with an open mind and focus on the content of his words. Jesus has chosen to speak to all who are willing to listen. Let his words be an inspiration to all who read them.

What Did He Really Say?

I always wondered what it would have been like to be able to have heard one of his ministries when he walked the earth. In one of our sessions with our Lord, I asked him if he would give us a message that he would have given the people. Here are his words:

> *I told them of the love of God for each and everyone. If you love God, there is nothing to fear; your soul will join me in heaven. If you create or act in an evil fashion, your soul will not progress in the realms of heaven. Spread the words of God and you will find peace. Death is not the end but the beginning of a new life with me in heaven. Hurt others and your soul will have to pay the price, and your judgment will not be good. God loves all; it is that simple! If you love others as God loves you, your soul will be with me in heaven. That is pretty much the message that I gave when I was on Earth.*

His words spoken 2,000 years ago certainly apply to present times. We had channeled with him multiple times in private as I wrote the book *Spirits Speak: Channeling the Life of Jesus*, but on February 12, 2018, we did our first Facebook Live event for the Words of God Then and Now group, where the public could listen as we received his words and decide for themselves if we were actually communicating with our Lord. Here is his first public message:

> *You have been brought together to hear my words. You have a special place in my heart. You are to go forth and make others hear my words as well. Tonight is a very special night! This is the first time I have spoken to you. Be not afraid to speak of me as you talk to others. My words of love are for all to hear. These are times when the strength of Satan is growing. It must be stopped. If all of you heed my words, it will make a difference. This group is special; all were called for this mission. God's love is infinite and with you at all times. It is up to each of you how you want to live your lives. If you love God and have no fear of death, you will be with me in heaven. Barry is my son and speaks my words. Connie was a trusted follower and also speaks for me. All of you are special and have loved me in the past. The future is uncertain. That is why you need to spread my words. I have blessed all of you tonight. With that blessing comes responsibility. You are my messengers. Go in peace and know that I am with you always. God bless you all.*

In that message, he defined the theme of what was to come in subsequent messages, namely, that it is a time of growing evil and he wanted those listening to spread his words.

Jesus Speaks of the Future

Later in the month, he came to us again as he spoke again to us on Facebook Live.

> *You are all here tonight to hear my words. Know I am always with you. There are times that you will doubt my presence, but I am still with you. Know, as well, my commands. There will be peace, but that peace will be in heaven. Go forth and speak my words and know that you will find that peace with me. You are speaking my words, and you will continue to do my bidding. In the next days, there will be*

much grief. Do not worry; much good will come soon. All who believe in me will be fine. Those who do not believe will have to suffer the consequences. Have faith, and all will be fine. Do not fear; I am with you. Have love in your hearts and love God.

In this session, he reiterated that he wanted the group members to spread his words but spoke of a time of grief that would be coming in the days ahead. He also said that those that believe in him have nothing to fear.

He returned to us again in March with this message:

You are here tonight to once again hear my words. Trust in God, and all things are possible. You are all very special people and have known me in prior lives. Your words are special when you speak of me. My love for you is unending and can never be broken. When you speak of me, your words can help drive out Satan. His strength is growing, and you must help my mission to stop his evil. When you speak of me, his power is diminished. God always wins; there is no doubt. Keep my love for you in your hearts; that is your protection. Those that do not have that love will perish. Soon there will be a time when your faith will be tested. Please know that I will be with you through that time, and when it is over, there will be a time of peace and goodwill.

This was the second time that he alluded to something that was going to happen that would bring grief to our country. I asked him if he would give us more detail about the time that was approaching. He replied:

No; that is defined by karma, and nothing will change it. You must not fear; I am the way and the light. With me, all will be fine. Without me, a time of grief will take place.

As this book goes to press, our country has gone through the experiences associated with the COVID-19 pandemic and riots in the streets. While many have suffered from this virus and there have been many deaths, he tells us that this was not the time of grief referred to in the previous writing. When we asked him for clarification, we were told that the time of grief would be a natural event. He is quite emphatic that all who love God will be protected, from events either man-made or the doing of Mother Nature.

Message on Good Friday 2018

March 30, 2018, was Good Friday, and we were treated to a very special occasion. Jesus honored us with a Facebook Live session on the day that Christians have chosen to remember his Crucifixion and death. Here is his wonderful message:

You are here tonight to hear my words on the evening when we remember my death. Know that I am risen from the dead and am with you at all times. Be aware that many would not accept that I am resurrected from the dead. Many will preach that I do not love all of you; that is not true. I love each and every one of you. We must join together in defeating evil. Satan is growing every day. He must be defeated, or humans will cease to evolve. I want all of you tonight to pray to me for help in defeating Satan. There is much evil in the world today, and many fail to realize what is happening. Your politicians are trying to take God away from you. If this happens, all will be lost. Your president is trying to stop this from happening, but he is in danger of losing. If that happens, all will lose as well. Now is the time to stand up for God. I tell you this because I want your country to prosper. Your country is the closest to my teachings. I helped found your country years ago; now your country is in danger of losing my blessings. My desire is for your country to prosper. Without God, you will fail. It is not too late. _

All of you have been brought together because you have been with me before. I tell you this before it is too late. Greed has taken over your government. You must return to God. Greed will destroy all. Love for one another will save you. Please heed this warning and bring God's word back to all. This is why Barry and Connie were sent back; they will continue to bring you my words. Keep the love of God in your hearts and speak of this love. I want you to hear these words on this special evening.

I died so that you would remember me and the words that I taught. Those words have been distorted through the years. I taught a very simple message of love—not fear—but if that message of love is lost, the future of man is in question. Please pray that my words will be heard and believed. I bless all of you on this special evening. I will now leave you, but I am always here for you. In your prayers tonight, ask for God to bless your country as well. Go in peace and love! Amen!

The Procession to Calvary – Ridolfo Ghirlandaio – cc1505 – The National Gallery, London, UK

Truly an inspiring message on the evening when Christians around the world commemorate his death. He is quite emphatic about the growth of evil and what greed is doing to our country.

A Mission for All of Us

In April, he came to us with the following words:

Go forth and know that you are doing my bidding. There is much to do, and I have entrusted you with this mission. God tries to love all, but there is so much evil in the world today. Know that things must change. How that happens is in the hands of a few. You are part of the few. Together, you must spread my words. Love is the only answer. It will not be easy. Many will ridicule you and vilify your words. I want you to know that you will succeed with my help. Never feel that you are alone.

He was making it clear that everyone hearing his words was expected to take his message of love to others and that the evil that was growing would destroy our country if not stopped. In early May, he returned once again for a live internet session.

I am here tonight to once again tell everyone of my love for each and every one of you. As we begin to advance on your mission, I want you all to know that you will succeed with my help. We are currently undergoing many acts of evil that are threatening to tear us apart. You must not let that happen. Love is always the answer! There is much hatred among many people. That hatred will destroy them, and they will have wasted a valuable lifetime. When they return home to me in heaven, they will have to pay for that hatred. They will have wasted a life plan. They will have to repeat that learning experience again. Those of you that have love for me in your hearts will advance in my kingdom. It is truly that simple. When I walked the earth, I also experienced such hatred. Nothing has changed. That is why I sent you back at this time. Barry and Connie were sent back to lead you and provide you with my words; together we will not lose. Together we will defeat the powers of Satan! Know that I will not allow failure in this mission. Know also that you are special in my eyes; many of you have served me when I walked the earth. Many of you were my devoted followers who spread my words and were persecuted for your actions. Know that I appreciate and love you for your past actions, but the time is now here for additional actions: Without your help, much will be lost! With your help, much will be gained! These are my words for you tonight! Go forth with my blessings, and know that you will succeed! Amen!

Many of the individuals listening to the live messages were sent back to help spread his message of love at a very critical time in the history of man. This time has been selected because technology has enabled man to annihilate humans on the earth, but that same technology can be used to spread the words of love and faith. If greed and hatred do not end, our evolution is in danger.

More Messages about Satan and Love

At the end of May, he returned to us once more.

I am here to bring all of you my message of love and hope in your future. As I speak here tonight, much is happening in your world. Satan is very active and will win without your actions. What I wish for you to do is to spread my messages as I speak them through Barry and Connie. They have been sent back for this purpose; they speak my words and know of my plans. Each of you are brought here to know that you are special in my eyes and heart. It is all of you that will force Satan to lose. Tonight is the beginning of your ministries, and you must know that you will succeed. All must know my love and spread those words. God always wins! There may be times when you doubt my presence, but I am always with you and hear your prayers. God will bless and keep every one of you here tonight.

Many are doubting my presence and speak that there is no God. They will have to bear my wrath and will have wasted a lifetime. I am the way and the light of the world!

You will have everlasting life in the upper realms if you speak my words. Those that speak that God does not exist will also have everlasting life but will spend it in the lower realms. Their lives will remain unfulfilled in heaven, while those that speak my words will enjoy the bounties of my love and will live in the magnificence of my upper realms. I and my closest followers and disciples live in the upper realm, where we attempt to guide souls and teach that all can become like God. Know that I will be the way to being like God. Tonight you must all take a strong step toward spreading my words. Much is at stake if the people do not heed my warnings; your evolution is in danger. Speak to all that will listen. Tell them they must believe in me as the way forward. If Satan is allowed to flourish, as is the current case, all the years of positive evolution will be wasted. The future for humans can be bright with my guidance, but if evil continues to flourish, the future of humans will be in doubt. I love and bless each one of you here tonight. You are my modern disciples, and I love each of you as I loved those that walked the earth with me. Go in peace and know that I walk with you as well.

Transfiguration – Raphael – cc1520 – Pinacoteca Vaticana, Vatican City.

After this session, we began to conduct channeling sessions with other holy spirits, such as Saint Paul, Saint Peter, Saint Thomas, John the Baptist, and others, in preparation for the information contained in this book. At the beginning of August, when I asked who he wanted for the next interview and subsequent chapter in this book, he replied that he wanted to do the next live event. On August 8, he delivered this message on Facebook Live:

> *I am here tonight because I have a very important message for all of you. I want you all to know that I love every one of you and hear all of your prayers. Tonight I want to stress how important it is that each one of you try to bring my messages to others. This is a time of great evil. Satan is very active and is winning in many areas. Many families have no father and have abandoned the church, while some of what is taught in church is not accurate to my words. Please keep in mind that it is the best reference you have concerning my teachings. I am trying to let all know my true teachings through Barry and Connie; they were sent back by me to bring you these messages. Those of you in the group know that you as well have a special relationship with me. You've been sent back as well to spread my words; without you much will be lost. With you all is possible. My words of love are everlasting and will bring comfort to those suffering and in grief. Without my presence, all would be lost. Together we will succeed where others have failed. Tonight will mark a beginning for many. All who listen must believe that you are actually hearing the words of God. Jesus when he walked the earth was God incarnate, and the words that I spoke were those of God. Be not afraid to speak my words; your reward will be when you return home with me in heaven. Those that refuse to listen to my words will not enjoy the fruits of heaven but will have to return and repeat the lessons they failed to learn. Love is the answer, and many live by hate, and that is not the answer. Those that live by hatred and speak against the existence of God will not do well when they face my judgment. Please remember that I am with all of you; my strength will be your strength to lead others to my love. Do not fear the words of others that will criticize you. They criticized me, but my words are still with you after 2,000 years. Bringing people to know me is your ultimate goal. I want to thank all of you for what you have accomplished. It will soon be apparent what my plan is for all of you. Soon my words will be published in Barry's book and*

be there for all to see. When you become aware of the big picture, you will be pleased and proud to have participated in bringing people to God.

In September, I asked Laura, our master guide, who Jesus wanted us to interview during our next Facebook Live session. She replied that Jesus had a special message and would do the next interview himself. On September 19, after signing on for the show, I asked if our Lord was with us and had a message. Here is his message from that session:

Yes, I am here once again to bring all the listeners my words of faith and love. As those of you know that have listened before, I speak of the growing strength of Satan. It is becoming more and more evident every day, especially in your government. I hope that all of you will follow your heart and send individuals to Washington that love me and will work for your country. Your future depends on major changes being made for your government. I want all of you here tonight to know that hatred is not going to help you advance in the realms of my heaven. I taught love, and love is what will help you to progress when you are home with me. It makes me very sad to see all the hatred being exhibited today. How anyone can imagine they are following my preaching's when they spew such hatred is unimaginable. I watch what is happening, and it breaks my heart. It is up to you, the members of this group, to spread my message of love and peace for all. Tonight is a very special night for all of you, as I will now bless each and every one watching tonight! My blessings are with you and will continue to lighten your pathway; do not ever think that I have abandoned you. I am always with you, and you will be aware of my presence. In the near future, I will make it apparent that these are my words and they are meant to guide and teach you of my true teachings. Barry's book about my life is available. That book tells the truth of my time on Earth and what I truly spoke. When you read that book, you will become more aware of how much I love each one of you. Until that time, I will have my closest souls speak to you through Barry and Connie, and they will bring you messages that were spoken by me. Soon it will be very important that all of you have no doubts that these are my words; much depends upon you. I have arranged for some questions and I will now answer.

In November 2018, we conducted a channeling session with the Blessed Mother Mary on Facebook Live. At the end of the session, Jesus came through and gave us a message.

Tonight you heard words of love from my mother. Her spirit watches over all of you, as does mine. You are special in my eyes, because many of you have served me in many other lifetimes. There are many of you that are new to my service. Know that it is possible to gain status in heaven by following my teachings. Each lifetime that you devote to my words will contribute to your advancement in heaven. There is much evil around you; you must fight that evil. Know that many of the politicians do not care what happens to you; they only care about power and greed. There is much evil in your capital and in your government. If that evil is not stopped, your country is in danger! I founded the United States as the country most close to my teachings. You have wandered from my original teachings, and if you do not return, there will be a penalty. Your evolution is in your own hands. I love each and every one of you, even those that don't understand my love. In the future, I will take a more active role in bringing you messages and instructions. There will be no doubt in the future that you are hearing my words. Barry and Connie will continue to bring the words to you, and Barry will be given powers of healing from me to prove that he is truly my messenger and son. I want all of you to go in peace tonight. God has blessed each one of you. Tonight has been special! I and my mother have been able to speak of our love. Go in peace and know that my love for you will never end. God bless you and keep you. Amen.

A Message for Christmas

As we approached the Christmas season, we received a message for all as the world began the celebration of his birth. Here is that message:

Good evening, tonight I want to come to you in this season when we celebrate my birth. Through the years, the celebration has become more and more commercialized and less of the devotion to God, as it was intended. Tonight I would like to bless every one of you that are listening and want you to know that when I walked the earth, I spoke of love for one other. Today your world is filled with evil and with those that have greed in their hearts. In order to bring my words to all of you, you must pay attention to what is spoken here tonight. When I walked the earth, I spoke simply of love of one another and of devotion to God. Those of you that pay attention to those words will join me in my heaven. I want all of you here tonight to know the love that is in my heart for all of you. This should be a time of special devotion! It should be a time when you gather with your family and you give thanks for all the blessings you have. It should not be a time to delve into the negative things in your lives. It should be a time for happiness and goodwill and cheer. Remember that when I lived, I was sent to Earth as a small baby. My birth is what you celebrate here today. In my life, I tried to spread words of love and hope for everyone! Please bring that hope forward and make this a time where you dedicate your lives to helping others, to spreading the love that I tried to spread, and to eliminating the hatred that many feel for one another. Go forward on this evening and know the power of the one God. Know that I speak for God and for the time that I walked the earth as Jesus. It is a time of goodwill and cheer. It is a time of meditation and a time to show your love for all those around you. With those words, I will bless you and I will leave my countenance upon you, and may you have a wonderful Christmas holiday and bring forth the love that I feel for you to others.

In the beginning of February 2019, we conducted a channeling session where I asked questions that were submitted by the members of the Words of God Then and Now Facebook group. At the end of the event, Jesus came through with this message:

I want to thank all of you individuals for listening to the questions that have been answered tonight. I want all of you to know that I watch over you. I understand your problems, and I will give you guidance toward understanding what I expect of you and what you can do to fulfill my teachings and to spread the love that I preached when I walked the earth and that I still try to guide all of you into doing. Evil is rampant at the current time, and it is a time for action! You will know the truth of my life in the near future. As you see and understand the happenings of my life, you will understand the love that I have shown in life as Jesus and from the other side as the power of God. Please go forward and try to spread my words of love, knowing that many will not pay attention. When I walked the earth, it was obvious that many thought I was crazy and they would not follow, and as you now know, my words have lasted for thousands of years. It is possible that your words and teaching can have a lasting impact on others for a long period of time as well. Together we will accomplish this mission of love. Continue to listen to the words that I give my son and Connie. They speak my words, they speak my truths, and they speak of my love for all. Tonight I bless you; I will continue to bless you and watch over you. I know each and every one of you, I know what is in your hearts, and I know that you mean well. With these words, I will leave you for tonight. Please live the love that I feel for you. Amen.

Faith, Politics, and Abortion

In February of 2019, Jesus requested that we do a special Facebook Live session so he could bring his message to the people. Here is his message:

You have scheduled this evening as I have requested of you, and I am happy to see that many of your members and followers are joining in to listen tonight to my words.

First of all, I want all of you in the group to know how proud that I am of you and of your service to me and your attempts in spreading my words. I realize that it is a very difficult task that you are facing; many out there will never believe that Barry is truly speaking my words. You can rest assured that he is indeed saying my words. Unfortunately, there are those out there that do not believe in me or that have been indoctrinated in the belief that every word that has been written about me and that appears in the gospels is the truth. Now that the book about my life is out, you will all be aware of the events that shaped my life. You will learn that I lived and loved as any other human would have lived and loved. My life was very normal for many years until I began my ministries and began to conduct miracles, which were intended to prove to the people that I was truly a very special person. I told people that I was the Son of God, even though I was God incarnate! It would have been impossible for the people that listened to my words to believe that I was truly God. I had been sent back to prove to them and to tell them that there was only one

God. At the time I returned, they worshipped many, so I felt it would not have been to the advantage of my message to tell them that I was truly God and have them mix me up with the other ones they were worshipping at the time.

I want you all to know that many of you have been sent back to help spread my words. As my messages become more and more apparent, it should become easier for you to find those who have room in their hearts to understand my message and to know I spoke a very simple message of love when I walked the earth.

In the very near future, things will begin to happen to make it much easier for you to spread my words. The beginning is the availability of my book. The words that Barry has written in my book are those that I have told him to write. I had my closest spirits come through and assist him with the information that he will be presenting to you. Now that the information is available, I ask that each of you take time to read it and understand it. What you will see in the book is contrary to what you have been led to understand in the gospels that were selected for the Bible. Know this: what you read in that book you can believe, because they are truly my words; this will be but the start of a large campaign to bring people to understand my simple message. It will only be after the people understand just how innocent and loving my experience on Earth was that they can pass on that love to others. Those others will in turn pass on my message of love, and so should begin a very large movement of leading people back to equal respect and love for one another.

At the present time, your politicians are leading you down a very evil path. They have become more accustomed to greed and wealth than to looking out for the people of your country. When I worked with your founding founders, I laid out principles that could live and work for millennia. Many of those principles have been misinterpreted and changed so as to put the long-term existence of your country in danger. They must return to the founding principles! They must learn that the best interests of the people of your country are foremost. When you vote for your politicians, you must ask them if they can conform to my preachings.

One very important lesson that I will leave with you tonight is the sanctity of life for the innocent before they are born. Abortion is a terrible sin! Those that perform abortions are contrary to my preachings in the worst sort of way. It is possible that things can go wrong, and there are exceptions, but in most cases, the innocents that are killed in the womb have had their life plans shortened for no reason. You must understand that life is a most valuable asset. When you are sent back, your soul enters the womb with a path that has been selected for you alone. You have chosen lessons that must be learned, you have chosen sorrow that you must grieve for, and perhaps you even selected loneliness, because it is a lesson your soul has to learn. When the innocent are destroyed, life plans are destroyed as well, and the soul must go back and create an entirely new life plan, and their path to rising in the realms of my heaven has been disrupted.

Use common sense as you select your elected officials; think of what I taught the founding fathers and attempt to select those that speak of those ideals. Your country is truly at risk; that is one reason why I have selected this time to send back Barry and Connie, as well as many of you that are listening. I will give you the information and tools to work with; use those tools wisely. Barry has been given the gift of healing, and when he heals others, it will add as proof that he truly speaks my words, just as I gave the gift of healing to the others of my disciples and others through time that spoke for me.

At this time, I would like to bless each and every one of you that are listening. I know each of you, and I know that each of you carries my love in your heart. Your mission is not easy, but if you persevere with my help, you will succeed. With those words, know that you are blessed, know that you carry my love in your hearts, and know that all will be fine. Go in peace and bring my message of love to others.

In March of 2019 Jesus came through for us once again and gave us a prediction for the future.

Yes; I want to bless each one of you that listened to this message. I want you to study the information that is available to you. Once you totally understand my teachings and what it means to love me, it will be much easier for you to go forward and attempt to bring my message to others. You are a special group of people. I have brought you together for a purpose; that purpose is to spread my words, to teach my true meanings, and to convert others to having love for me in their hearts. It is not an easy assignment; when I walked the earth, there were times that I was very frustrated, and individuals swore at me and called me crazy and would do things. There will be a time it will be very obvious you are hearing my messages and my words. That time is rapidly approaching. With those words, I want you to know that I love you and that I am with every one of you. I bless you all tonight. Have me in your hearts, have me in your minds, and have me in your prayers. With those words, I will say good night and amen!

Christ Crucified – Diego Valazquez – 1632 – Museo del Prado, Madrid, Spain.

Message on Good Friday 2019

Tonight, I want you to know that I am God, and as God, I love each and every soul that walks your planet! Many of you have doubts that Barry and Connie actually speak my words. Tonight I want to assure you that the words that Barry is speaking are the words of God. On this night many years ago, I died on a cross; I died on that cross so that I would be remembered and so that I could resurrect from the grave and prove to all the wonderful powers of our God. The proof of resurrection is the greatest miracle that was ever performed on your planet. At a time in the future, it may be necessary that I perform another miracle to prove to all that these are truly my words. For this time, please focus on what I am to tell you.

As true as I rose from the grave, each and every human will pass from the earth, and their souls will enter my heaven. The position of your souls in my realms of heaven will depend upon how you show your love for others and your love for yourself. If you have my love in your hearts, your souls will progress in my realms! If you follow the words that are spoken by Barry and Connie, you can rest assured that all will be well when you pass from your human lifetime and come home into my heaven. Please know that your death, which is inevitable, is not the end of your soul journey but only the beginning of a new one. Just as my body died on the cross and my soul entered into heaven, so will your souls enter into my heaven as well.

Please take your time that I have allotted you to walk the earth to pass on my words of love to your family and your neighbors and to attempt to lead lives that will make me proud. There is much evil on your planet today. That is why I have been sending back the souls of my closest followers. I have sent back to you one of my closest followers in the body of Mother Teresa. I have sent back to you one of the reincarnated souls of my sons when I walked the earth in the form of Reverend Billy Graham, and I have other very special souls speaking to you tonight. They were sent back with a specific mission; Barry and Connie are doing their best to fulfill the role that I sent them back to fulfill. My book telling the story of my life is currently available to you. Barry is completing another book that will tell you the messages and stories of my disciples and of my current messages. There will be a third book that tells of my teachings. Those three books will give you a true foundation of what I teach and what I know will help you to progress in the realms of heaven.

On this evening thousands of years ago, I suffered and passed from your planet. I did so that I could rise from the grave and prove to all that the power of God is all supreme, and with the power of God all is possible. Please hold this weekend holy. Please understand the tragedy of my death, as well as the miracle of my Resurrection. Know that it all happened. Know that you have been given the actual details of what took place; also know on this very special evening that I bless each and every one of you. Know that I am with all of you. Know that if you are suffering, I am here to bring you comfort, and know that when your time is over, you will enter my heaven, and you will find that everything, all the pain, all the suffering that happened to you in your lifetime, will be past, and your future life in my realms will be indescribably wonderful! With these words of blessings and truth, I will now take a couple of questions that I have given Barry and Connie to ask. Just know that I love each and all of you and that I always will. Amen.

Messages concerning the Pandemic and Violence

On March 17 of 2020, the world was feeling the effects of the COVID-19 pandemic. Jesus came to us with a message concerning the crisis.

I have asked to speak with all of you tonight because I know that many of you are very fearful of what is taking place around you. It is something that none of you are used to. It is something that many of you are doubtful as to how it will end. I want to assure you tonight that I am watching over all of you. I am going to make sure that nothing will destroy your country or lead any of you to ever doubt my presence. I love each one of you. I watch over all of you, and I especially hear your prayers to me. Know that your prayers are heard!

I will make sure that even though there will be many that suffer, the effects of this virus will be minimal. Your country is undergoing an emergency that has been started by others that are enemies of your great United States. Others know that the United States represents the principles that I instilled in your founding fathers. There are other countries that fear that your country will remain the shining star that leads the world in freedom of religion, speech, and the many things that all of you hold dear.

I know that all of you are currently suffering. Many of you fear that you will be unemployed; many of you fear that it will affect members of your family. I want to assure you that what your government is doing will pay dividends in the long run. You will all go through a time of uncertainty with this, but it will be relatively short. What you must do is learn to love your neighbors, help those that need help, be firm in standing for your principles, and let others come to you for advice.

It will do you no good to have worry in your hearts. That worry will lead to despair and a feeling that you have no control over the events that are taking place. There will be a time, in the not-too-distant future, where your lives will return to normality. Just know that your love for me will be your protection! Pray to me! Pray to my archangels! Pray to my holy saints that serve me! Many of these spirits have come through for you in the past with their messages. You can go back and listen to these wonderful messages, and you will get a better understanding of how your world is cared for, watched and blessed over, by all of these holy forms. Use this time that you have to repair family relationships that have been strained in the past. Use this time to reaffirm your faith in God. All of these things will pay benefits for you in the future. Drive hatred from your heart, and know that all will be well.

I hope my words have served to be a calming influence for you tonight. I can come forward to you in the future should I feel it is necessary. You are approaching the time that you celebrate my death and my Resurrection. This is a very important time not only for Christianity but for other religions. I want all of you to practice the love that I showed when I walked the earth. So I hope that with these words, I have been able to help you understand that your future is not as dark as it looks at this time. So I am now going to leave you. Know that I have blessed each and every one of you. I hope that you have felt my loving energy tonight, and I hope that I have been able to instill a confidence that all will truly be well for you. So with these words, I am going to say good night. God has blessed all of you, and he will continue to bless all of you in the future, and God is your protection, and God is your way forward out of this time of stress.

By July of 2020, many troubling events were taking place in the United States. Continuing fear of the pandemic, riots and violence in the streets, and a widening political divide were driving people apart. On July 5, 2020, Jesus returned with another message concerning the troubling events.

What you are currently seeing, and what is going on in the world around you, is quite troubling. As we watch from the other side, we can see that evil is transforming much of the good that people had been able to accomplish in their history.

There have been times that your country has undergone terrible attempts to undermine and to overthrow all of the good that has taken place since I worked with your founding fathers to form the United States. There have been many times of danger. You had civil war. You had riots, and you have had strife. Today the dangers that are facing your country are much different. Many people have turned away from me. In your schools, it is often taught that I do not exist and that my powers are nonexistent. I want to assure you that that message is incorrect. Just as I am here to speak to you tonight, I have attempted to lead your people for the hundreds of years since you first came into existence. My teachings are of love for one another, are of love for me, and of love for your country. There are those that are trying to destroy the United States. There are those that are seeking power and greed and who wish to have all of the wonderful accomplishments of your country forgotten.

It is a time for people to turn back to relying upon their love for me. It is a time for people to stand up to evil as they see it, and it is a time for all to step forward and make their voices heard. Hopefully, many will look at what is taking place in your country and will understand that even though all of you are equal in my eyes, there are none that are more supreme than any other. I created all the races that you have on this earth. I did it as part of the challenge that people will face to find love for those that are a different color, of a different race, or speak a different language. All those different characteristics are capable of generating hatred among the people. It is very important that you do what I have told you to do. Do not fall for the promise of a utopia or a world in which law enforcement does not exist. It is written in the gospels, "Blessed are the peacemakers." That is accurate to my teachings! There must be those that serve others. There must be those that care for others. Just as evil walks the earth, so must those that care for others walk the earth as well.

I want you to look deeply into your hearts. Understand how your love for me affects your lives. Do not fall into the trap of having violence toward others because you feel that the words that others are speaking are the truth. If the words that others are speaking are contrary to the words that I spoke, do not follow them. Know that my very simple teachings of love, if taken to heart by all, will lead to a world where all wonderful things can happen. What is necessary is for people to understand that it is only the love for me that will make a positive evolution possible. Go forward and tell others that acts of violence are never part of my teachings. Know that sometimes violence is needed to protect the weak; know that violence can be needed to protect the innocent. But never promote violence for bringing forth the objectives of evil. The history of humans has been a very difficult history. There have been terrible times throughout your history that violence and greed has caused great civilizations to fail. Know that violence and greed can destroy your country. It is up to each individual to voice their opinions and to pursue what they know is a way of living that follows my commands.

I have given humans free will, and I have given them egos. That is the test of how humans will evolve in the future. I sincerely hope that humans can grow in their love for me and that they will prosper and that through showing love for one another, be able to unite and to make a world where there is little poverty, where people can practice their religions, and where people can follow my words and know that is truly the way to successful evolution. I will be returning to you with more messages. Just know that I am with every one of you. I am hearing your prayers, and I understand how many of you are very distressed at the way things are happening. Pray to me and let me know that you are truly united with me in love and will tell others and hopefully affect others so that your evolution may continue. So with that, I am going to bless all of you that are listening to this. I want you to feel my loving energy, and I want you to know that absolutely you are not forgotten. You are going through a terrible time with this virus; things will improve. You have gone through difficult times in the past, and you have succeeded. This time will be no different. So with that, I am going to say good night. God bless. Keep your prayers coming to me, and together we will cure what is wrong in your world.

In this chapter, you got to read the contemporary words of our Lord, Jesus the Christ. He has brought us messages of love and forgiveness. As you read this chapter, a major fear he has for humanity is the growth of evil and growing away from God. He is also quite clear that he has allowed other cultures to self-destruct through the ages. Hopefully, humans will listen to his words before it is too late. It should now be apparent that all you have to do is open your heart to his love, and all is possible.

CHAPTER 15

Constantine the Great

History knows Constantine the Great as the first Christian emperor of the Roman Empire and the individual to first make an attempt to organize the Christian religion. When he became emperor in AD 306, 275 years after the death of Christ, Christianity was in turmoil. Different groups argued whether Jesus was in fact a deity or just a prophet. There was even no agreement as to the date to commemorate his Crucifixion. As in the early days of Christianity, members of the faith were still being persecuted because of their faith.

Constantine the Great, the First Christian Roman Emperor – Adobe Stock

In the early years of his reign, Constantine competed for power with other emperors. In order to solidify his power, he had to defeat the other Roman factions. In AD 313, Constantine faced the forces of Maxentius at the Milvian Bridge over the Tiber River in Italy. According to accounts of his life, he had a vision that if he had a Christian symbol painted on the shields of his soldiers, he would be victorious. Constantine defeated Maxentius and entered Rome as emperor. Following his victory, he legalized Christianity and allowed freedom of worship in the Edict of Milan in AD 313.

The newfound freedoms for Christians resulted in more turmoil as different Christian factions tried to gain control, and in order to stop the unrest, in AD 325, Constantine summoned the leaders of the church to the Council of Nicaea. Out of this conference came the Nicene Creed, affirming once and for all that Jesus was a divine being. The conference also set the framework for the selection of gospels that would become the framework of the Bible.

Constantine believed that baptism would cleanse the body of sin, and only after he was near death did he allow himself to be baptized. He wanted to be as free of sin as possible when he faced judgment. His accomplishments were many, including ordering construction of the Church of the Holy Sepulchre in Jerusalem. Constantine is also criticized for selecting gospels for political expediency rather than those that truly depicted the life and teachings of Jesus.

His spirit appeared to us in channeling session, and here are his comments about the events of his life. Connie asked if he would like to begin with a message.

> *Yes; I want all of you to know that I am so happy to be with you today. It has been a long time since I had the ability to speak in front of other individuals and to be heard by so many. In my lifetime, I did the best I could to serve my Lord. I was in a position of power and was able to do things that other people cannot do. As you will see from the questions that are going to be asked, I believe that I was actually quite successful in furthering the cause of Christianity in the world. So, thank you! Thank you for having me, and thank you for the honor of allowing me to answer these questions.*

That was quite a humbling statement, coming from an individual whose influence on the Christian faith may be second only to Jesus.

His Beginnings

Constantine was born into a military and powerful family in the later AD 280s. His father, Flavius Valerius Constantius was a high-ranking army officer that was raised to the rank of Caesar, or deputy emperor, in AD 293. Constantine was raised at the court of the senior emperor, Diocletian, in what is now modern Turkey. His mother, Helena, played a large role in his life. Connie asked Constantine if his mother was a Christian.

Mother was a believer in Jesus; she heard the stories of him, but he had died 200 years before she was born, so the only information she had were the stories that were being told about him. But yes, she was a Christian.

"So were you raised a Christian?"

In those days, you had to pretend that you were following the Roman edict, so there were times we had to pretend we were following the pagan gods of Rome, but yes, I always believed that I was a Christian.

"Why did you convert to the Christian belief?"

I always felt in my heart that there was a true God. Mother always instructed me in the fact that there was a single God. The Jews actually had that belief, and as Romans, we put up with the Jewish population. I always felt that my soul was closer to the Christian God than it was to the pagan gods, and messages and visions that I had in my head verified it for me.

"What role did your mother play in founding the Christian church?"

As my power became more complete, she played a huge role. She went to Jerusalem and oversaw the beginning of the construction of the Church of the Holy Sepulchre, among other things. She was a very valuable ally in spreading the word of God.

"Did you believe that you had a personal relationship with God?"

Yes; I always felt from the visions in my head and the messages I was receiving that I had a personal relationship with God, and that relationship is what helped give me strength in what I did. As I gained more power, I actually began to feel that I was a true apostle of our Lord.

"Did you have psychic abilities?"

I did not realize it at the time, but I did have the ability to hear messages in my head and to see visions in my mind. Now that I am over here and understand much better what was taking place, I know that I did have psychic abilities, just as you and Connie have.

From this answer, it should be obvious that he did not believe psychic abilities were tantamount to witchcraft!

Formal Conversion

Prior to Constantine's rise to power, he served in various capacities in the Roman army. Emperor Diocletian, the ruler during this period of time, actively persecuted Christians. We inquired if Constantine ever participated in the murdering of Christians.

Sadly, I had to observe and follow orders, but I never ordered or murdered Christians on my own.

"When were you converted to Christianity?"

In the beginning, I served in the military, and it was very difficult to profess my true beliefs, so it was not until I started to truly gain power that I made it public that I was a Christian. In the beginning, as I said, I showed others that I worshipped the pagan gods so that I could further myself in the Roman army.

"So how exactly did the conversion take place?"

As I said, I always believed in God, and as I gained strength and power, others could not challenge me in my beliefs, so I just started to profess Christianity more and more. There was a time that I had enough power and ability to proclaim that Christians were no longer going to be persecuted.

"Was your conversion politically motivated?"

No, not at the time. It was a personal thing for me. I did realize as I gained power that the Christians were gaining in strength as well, and by following my heart and my mind and stopping the persecution of Christians, it would also be politically favorable to the continuance of Roman power.

It was a basic teaching of the Christian religion that baptism cleansed the soul of sin. The writings about the life of Constantine indicate that he declined baptism until he was essentially on his deathbed. Connie asked him why he was not baptized at an early age.

I understood that baptism cleans one's body of one's sin. I knew that as emperor of Rome, I would have to give orders that perhaps were against the ultimate will of God. I wanted to wait until later in life so that all of my sins would be cleansed. I felt that if I did it early, the orders that I had to carry out after baptism would be held against me.

An interesting concept! I want to assure the reader that being baptized on your deathbed does not redeem the soul for a life of evil.

Rise to Power

During this time, the Jewish religion had a large following in the Roman community. Connie inquired as to his opinion of the Jewish faith.

I knew that the Jews followed a belief different than those of the Romans, and I knew that most of the converts to Christianity were also members of the Jewish faith. So I honored their traditions and beliefs but did not feel they had the whole story correct.

Constantine's rise to power involved many military conflicts that defeated those with whom he had initially shared power. His greatest victory came against Maxentius at the Battle of the Milvian Bridge in October, AD 312. We asked what sign he saw before he went into battle.

Before I went into battle, I had this vision that if I took Christian symbols and put them on the shields of my soldiers, that we were going to be victorious. As you know, that turned out to be true.

This was the last major military engagement in his quest for power, and after it was over, Constantine entered Rome as supreme emperor. In less than a year after assuming power, he issued the Edict of Milan in AD 313, attempting to allow freedom for all religions in the Roman Empire. Connie asked why he issued this edict.

I kept receiving this message that we needed to stop the persecution of Christians; I basically tried to have freedom of religion for all Romans. I protected the Christians, but in order not to have any uprising among the people that still had pagan beliefs, I also gave them freedom of religion as well.

"What was your opinion of Arianism?"

I felt that Arianism was wrong; that was one reason why I wanted to call the masters of the church together at Nicaea. We needed to resolve once and for all what was going to be the true path of Christianity in the future.

First Council of Nicaea

After the Edict of Milan in 313, the different factions in the Christian church were literally at war. They were fighting among themselves, and the Romans feared the situation could get out of control and weaken the empire. It was nearly 300 years since the death of Christ, and they could not even decide what date to celebrate Easter. In AD 325, Constantine decided to call the hierarchy of the church together in the town of Nicaea to establish some ground rules for the future of the church. We asked him why he decide to convene the First Council of Nicaea.

There were multiple reasons. At that time, Christianity was pretty much in turmoil. Easter was being celebrated at different times of the year; the Arians were trying to lead the church in a separate direction. There were people following agnostic teachings that I felt were not correct. So I felt that by pulling all the powerful members of the church together in one conference, we could attempt to resolve some of the problems and divisions that the church was facing.

"How many of the bishops of the church attended?"

There were around 300, as I recall.

"What role did Nicaea play in the selection of the gospels?"

When I called the conference of Nicaea, it was 300 years after the death of Christ. Unfortunately, much of the writings that we were reading at the time were based on stories and myths. I needed to try to give the church direction and decide on its path. The gospels we were looking at, and there were many of them, were incomplete. We tried to simplify all of the teachings that were available and try to decide the path. We came up with what you folks refer to as the Nicaea creed, which laid the basis of what we felt the foundational teachings of the church should have been.

"Did any form of the New Testament exist before Nicaea?"

There had been attempts to put the books of the gospel together before Nicaea. There was much discussion about what should be included and should not be included. One thing that we did determine at the conference was that the senior members of the church and the bishops would attempt to determine what gospels would be included in the Bible that would enforce the words that we spoke of in the Nicaea creed.

"How many gospels were in the Bible?"

At the time, as I remember, we had somewhere around 26.

"What role did you play in selecting the gospels that would go into the Bible?"

They would come to me, and I would either approve them or disapprove them. I actually played a fairly large role in the selection of what you see in your gospels today.

"Why were the gospels of Matthew, Mark, Luke, and John selected but those of Thomas, Mary, and others deleted?"

We considered the books of Thomas, Mary, and many others as agnostic gospels, and we felt that agnosticism was not the true path that we wanted the church to follow. Matthew, Mark, Luke, and John were complete gospels at that time, all told pretty much the same story, and we felt that they should become key to the foundation of the church.

"Why were the agnostic gospels not selected?"

We felt that they did not represent the true path that we believe Jesus inferred in his teaching. I was also receiving what you would call psychic guidance on the path that God wanted us to follow.

"Were you familiar with the book of Revelation?"

Yes, I read Revelation, but it was so in contrast to what we wanted to pursue that I rejected it as being part of the original Bible.

"Who was most responsible for which gospels were selected for inclusion in the Bible?"

I had final decisions on it, but I attempted to rely on the most powerful bishops in the church for the recommendations.

One accomplishment of the Council of Nicaea was the creation of what we now refer to as the Nicene Creed. We asked if he was in complete agreement with the Nicene Creed.

No; the Nicene Creed represented a compromise. Keep in mind there were church members from the East and the West and that they represented many different viewpoints that they reflected because of the people that were in their congregations. They represented a compromise that I feel was a good compromise.

In order to understand how even the Nicene Creed has evolved, here is a translation based on the original Greek version. As you can see, it resolves the issue of whether Jesus was the Son of God.

We believe in one God,
the Father almighty,
maker of all things visible and invisible;
And in one Lord, Jesus Christ,
the Son of God,
begotten from the Father, only begotten;
that is, from the substance of the Father;
God from God,
Light from Light,
true God from true God;
begotten not made,
of one substance with the Father;
through whom all things came into being,
things in heaven and things on earth,
Who because of us men and because of our salvation came down;
and became incarnate
and became man,
and suffered,

and rose again on the third day,
and ascended to the heavens
and will come to judge the living and dead;
And in the Holy Spirit.
But as for those who say, there was when he was not;
and, before being born He was not,
and that he came into existence out of nothing,
or who assert that the Son of God is of a different hypostasis or substance,
or created,
or is subject to alteration or change
—these the Catholic and Apostolic Church anathematized. (https://christianhistoryinstitute.org)

Governing the Roman Empire

Shortly after the Council of Nicaea, Constantine made a decision that was to haunt him for the rest of his life. His son Crispus, from his first wife, Minervina, was accused of adultery by his second wife, Fausta. Historical details are unclear, but it is believed that Constantine ordered the death of his own son and ex-wife. We asked him to comment on what really happened.

I have never really wanted to talk about this; unfortunately, Crispus and his mother had an illicit relationship. I could not believe it when I heard the rumors, but when I investigated and found out it was true, I felt that such a sin would be punishable by the order of death.

Upon consolidating his power, Constantine accomplished much for the people of the Roman Empire. He decided to move the center of political power to a newly established city he named Constantinople. We asked him his motives for making such a great change. He replied:

I wanted a place that was remote from Rome. I wanted a place that would be unique and had a good seaport and a place that had the ability to grow in strength. I thought that the location I chose was a perfect location.

In spite of his moving the seat of political power, he chose Rome as the center of the Christian religion. Connie inquired why he made this decision.

There were more Christians in Rome than any other city under Roman rule. Many of the areas of the city on the outskirts had very few Christian followers.

"Did you feel that the bishop of Rome was the most powerful in the church?"

Well, Rome was the center of the Roman Empire and at the time the main seat of power in our world. The bishop of Rome had the largest number of followings, so I felt that Rome should become the center of the Christian religion.

"You legislated that Sunday should be a day of rest. Why did you do that?"

Keep in mind, at that time there were still many slaves and that people were being pushed and worked seven days a week. I realized that it was very harsh treatment, so I felt that it would be an order that would help everyone if they rested for one day during the week. It was not a religious act, but it was one that I thought made common sense.

"In AD 331, you commissioned 50 Bibles for the Church of Constantinople. How were the books of the Bible selected?"

By the time 331 came, we pretty much determined the gospels that would strengthen the foundation that we set forth in the creed. That pretty much covered the gospels that you see today. There have been many manipulations and changes in the wording of those gospels since we selected them. But by 331, we had a pretty good idea of what books we wanted to be included in the Bible.

In AD 337, Constantine fell ill and died after ruling for 31 years. His sons took over positions of power and ruled the empire for many years. On his deathbed, he finally was baptized, thinking all his sins would be absolved.

Constantine contributed much toward the growth of the Christian church. After listening to his interview, it became apparent that he had been sent back to spread and preserve the words of God, as had other souls before and after his life in the fourth century. We asked him if he is a member of the soul family of God. His response was this:

Yes; I have served Jesus many times before. He realized that by the time the fourth century was beginning that Christianity was having difficulties because of the persecutions of the Romans, so he sent me back to attempt to alleviate their suffering and to help Christianity advance.

"Did you feel that you were the successor of the apostles?"

Yes, I felt that. I realized through my messages and my mental images that it was time to stop the suffering of the Christians. I felt that I could serve our Lord as no other ruler previous to me was able to do. I made sure that Christians had the ability to worship without the fear of being martyred. Once that fear was taken away, the growth of the Church was inevitable.

"Can you add anything to explain your role in heaven?"

My role in heaven is trying to provide guidance to others. I work with the other holy spirit guides; I try to influence those in various religions that have power to influence others. I try to bring the love of God to as many as I can.

"Have you reincarnated since your life as Constantine?"

Yes; I have returned several times since my life as Constantine to serve our Lord. I came back around year 1,000, when the church was very much in disarray; unfortunately, my attempts at trying to bring reason to the church failed, and I returned once again as a church member in the 1300s and helped try to bring change to the church and make it more understandable for the people. So I have lived two lives since that of Constantine.

"Are you considering reincarnating again?"

When God wants me to return, I will certainly return. My soul has been in service to God for the millennia, and that will not change in the future. I am his servant, and I will do as he asks.

By establishing the seat of religious power in Rome, he laid the framework for the growth of the Catholic Church. Now that he is on the other side, he can see all that is and has happened within that religious organization. We sought his opinion on the modern Catholic Church.

I am very sad as I watch the Catholic Church today. It has been torn apart by priests and bishops that cannot follow the simplest order of decency and also watch as the pope attempts to bring some of his beliefs into what should be the most wonderful church in the world. The followers of the Roman Catholic Church are wonderful people; unfortunately, it's the members of the hierarchy that have created the problems for them. Hopefully, the church can be rebuilt and follow the true teachings of our Lord.

His opinion reflects the words of many of the holy spirits that have come forward to give us messages.

A Final Message

As we came to an end of our questions, it was apparent that we were speaking to a soul that has served God in many lifetimes. His actions truly did save Christianity from the cruelty of Roman rule and laid a foundation that allowed the words of Jesus to change the world. We asked this spirit of God if he had a final message.

Yes; I want to thank you for allowing me to come through today. In life I attempted to allow members of the Christian religion to worship without the fear of martyrdom. Before I came back, I watched with anguish from this side as individuals were killed and tortured in the most terrible ways. By me gaining power and becoming the emperor of Rome, I was in a position that my edicts would be listened to. After my passing, the hierarchy of Christianity attempted to reduce the effective-

ness of the Christian church, for which I was able to lay the foundation. I was able to create many churches throughout our country, and I feel that I did make a true lasting impact. I want all of you today to know that you are facing very dangerous times, as I faced. There is much evil in your world, and the difference is that evil has the ability to wipe out human evolution as you know it today through your weapons of mass destruction. You have to be strong, and you have to speak of the love of God. Without that, there will be no future for humanity. If you allow secularism to pull people away from their belief in God, you will find that, as all other civilizations have failed, your civilization will fail as well. With those words, I am going to leave you. God bless you, and thank you for allowing me to come through and answer your questions.

After having interviewed this incredible messenger of God, I believe it is truly possible that Constantine the Great is second only to Jesus in laying the foundation of the Christian church.

CHAPTER 16

Saint Augustine

Saint Augustine in His Study – Sandro Boticelli – 1480 – Church of Ognissanti, Florence, Italy.

When I started to write about Jesus and the holy spirits, we were told that Saint Augustine would provide information and guidance. At the time, I did not realize just how great his knowledge was or the amount of information he would provide. Also referred to as Saint Augustine of Hippo, his original name was Aurelius Augustinus. Born in current-day Tunisia in AD 354 to a well-to-do Roman family, he became one of the most influential writers about Christian doctrine and had a huge influence on the teachings of the Catholic Church. He based much of his work on the writings of Saint Paul. I was amazed to find out that over five million words of his writings survive. For comparison, this book will consist of around 73,000 words. Five million words is roughly equivalent to 69 of my books, and he did not have access to a computer! Augustine was a true intellectual giant, and his writings have had a momentous effect on religious teachings. We have been truly blessed to have the guidance of such an important, historic holy spirit.

His Message

We channeled with him on Facebook Live in September of 2018. Here is his opening message:

> *I am here to bring you the messages of God. Jesus has given me information that he wants me to pass to members of the group. He wants everyone to know that he is pleased with the progress you are all making and that he watches very closely what is taking place and is pleased that you are beginning to pass on his words. As he has told you before, Satan is gaining in strength, and you all need to help in passing on his words so that Satan can be defeated. Much evil exists in your political system today! There are those that are trying to overthrow the rule of law. God helped to form the United States and gave guidance to the founding fathers. Much of what your founders taught is being destroyed. If your country is to prosper, you must return to those original principles. The words in your Constitution are the words given to the founders by God; to go against those words will not be good for your country. Each of you must do your best to guide others to understand the importance of the teachings given by the founding fathers. Much has changed since your founding, but much needs to remain the same. God blesses the United States and hopes he can continue those blessings! Only the message of love for one another can provide a future guidance. Simply put, your citizens need to learn cooperation and love; without that, your future is in doubt. I will now answer your questions.*

At the time of writing this chapter, I have a very active Facebook group, Words of God Then and Now, and some of the members had suggested questions concerning the group. I started by asking Augustine if he felt the group was on the right path and starting to fulfill their goals. He replied:

> *Yes; they are learning and hearing the words of God through Barry and Connie. There will be many more messages in the future that will give all of them guidance. God blesses each and every one of those listening to his words.*

"What do you suggest the members of the group should do to be more effective in their learning and sharing?"

Each will contribute in their own way. For instance, Mary will be working with individuals in drug rehabilitation. Each one will find their own path. We will try to guide each of them and help them learn to understand messages from their guides.

For those of you unfamiliar with spirit guides, they are souls on the other side that are advanced in their learning, who attempt to guide humans in their actions. I wrote about spirit guides and how to communicate with them in my book *Afterlife: What Really Happens on the Other Side.*

A Future Plan

My age as I am writing this book is 77, and some of the members wondered what would happen when Connie and I will be unable to continue bringing them the messages. I asked Augustine what plan the spirits have for succession when Connie and I are unable to channel the messages. His response was this:

That part of the plan is already taking place. For instance, Sysco learned much about what is expected of her this week, the same way others will be informed. There will be others that will take your place. This is a long-term project that will take multiple lifetimes.

We had been told before that our future lives are already planned for us. Apparently, it is going to take quite a while for humans to understand the concept of loving one another. Many of our group members have small children and fear for their future. I addressed their worries by asking:

"There are a lot of bad things happening in the world today. What would be your message for those who have small children?"

They must learn to love God in their hearts. Those that love God have nothing to fear; he will take care of all that believe in him and help spread his words.

In an earlier session with Jesus, we were told that there would be a time of grief coming for our country but there was nothing to fear for those of us that have the love of God in our hearts. I asked Augustine if there was anything we should do to prepare ourselves spiritually or for our personal protection or that of our families.

Just have an unstoppable love of God in your heart. That will be your protection. Each of you will face the grief in different ways. Just remember that your love of God is your protection. Have no doubts!

We tried on several occasions to get a clue about the event that was coming, but none of the saints were going to give any details. Every time I bring up the subject, we are told that our protection is the love of God. Another fact concerning our soul journey is that we all have life plans before we enter an incarnate lifetime. When we began channeling, Augustine was one of the first of the high-ranking holy spirits to come through and give us information. He has proven to be a consistent source of information through the years. I asked him how long he had been aware of Connie's and my spiritual journey that has resulted in us being a spokesman for the holiest of spirits. He responded:

I helped with your life plan when you and Connie were on the other side. It was all part of the plan that I was to help you. Sometimes it was a little frustrating, but now your abilities have caught up with my guidance.

I can only guess how frustrated he was in the beginning when we were learning how to communicate with the spirits. Connie and I were certainly frustrated with our personal progress.

Soul Life before Augustine

I thought I would change the subject and ask some questions about his earlier lifetimes. In my next question, I asked if his soul ever walked the earth at the time Jesus walked the earth. He replied:

Yes, I was honored to have been a follower of Jesus. My name was Ethan. My role has been lost to history, but I was a faithful follower. I reincarnated as Augustine so that I could continue with the work of God.

"When Jesus walked the earth, what was your role in that lifetime?"

I supported the other disciples and tried to make notes of the words of Jesus. Unfortunately, my notes were destroyed.

In order for a soul to be as highly ascended as Augustine and to reach a level in the realms of heaven so close to God, his soul must have served God in many ways in many prior lifetimes. I asked him if he ever played a biblical role on Earth prior to the time Jesus walked the earth. He answered:

Yes, I also lived in the time of Moses and supported his work.

The soul of Augustine has been called on many times to support God. He has certainly been a faithful servant.

Life as Augustine

"Did you reincarnate as Augustine in the year AD 354?"

Yes.

"It is written that you were born in Africa. Where were you born?"

I was born in what is now Tunisia.

It is also written that Augustine was multilingual. I inquired as to the first language he learned to speak. He responded:

I learned Latin, since that was required by the Romans.

"Can you tell us about your teenage years?"

I did not follow the teachings of Christ in my early years.

Judging from some of his writings, he was a bit on the wild side in his early years. He lived with a woman and was the father of a son. I had run across a very interesting prayer that was attributed to a young Augustine. I asked if he really did utter the prayer, "Grant me chastity and continence, but not yet."

Unfortunately, yes. I was a little on the wild side in my youth.

I think many of us can look back and share his comment. His statement is proof that there is hope for all of us and that there really is a forgiving God. I inquired as to his opinion of Christianity during his early life.

I always believed in the one God, but physical pleasures were more important.

Testosterone obviously played a very important part in the early life of Augustine. My next question investigated into what caused him to convert to Christianity.

I received messages in my head that supported the one God.

He would have been born 29 years after the conference of Nicaea, where Emperor Constantine selected the gospels that would become the Bible and the official document of the Roman Catholic Church. I asked if, as he grew up, he was aware of the choices of gospels that were selected in AD 325 by Constantine.

Yes, but there were also many other works that have information about the life of Jesus. I tried to educate myself as much as possible.

"Did you ever question the gospels selected by Constantine?"

Yes, but it did little good. I knew from some of the other gospels that there were many different interpretations of the life and teachings of Jesus.

After the conference of Nicaea, many unanswered questions remained about the basic beliefs of Christianity. In an attempt to resolve some of the issues, the First Council of Constantinople was held in AD 381. Augustine would have been 27 years old at the time of the council. I asked him if he was invited to attend.

No, I was not invited. I was not totally dedicated to following God at that time of my life.

Conversion to God

When Augustine converted to following the teachings of God, he also converted to a life of celibacy. Considering his early history, this must have been a huge sacrifice. I asked him why he converted to a life of celibacy after having lived such a different youth.

I felt that sacrifice was required to make my life one with God. Celibacy was certainly a sacrifice for me.

"Do you still feel that celibacy is required to be close to God?"

No; I learned otherwise when I arrived home.

"Did you believe that Jesus was truly divine?"

Yes, I always believed that.

"Were you ever aware of the book of Revelation?"

Yes; it was very controversial, and I personally did not believe it.

"Did you ever write about reincarnation?"

No, that subject was decreed illegal by the Romans. Writings did exist publicly about it, but they were read privately.

The First Council of Constantinople redefined the words of the Nicene Creed. Here are the words of the Nicene Creed as defined at Constantinople in AD 381:

I believe in One God, the Father Almighty,
Maker of Heaven and Earth, and of all things visible and invisible. And in one Lord Jesus Christ, the Son of God, the Only-Begotten, begotten of the Father before all ages;
Light of Light; True God of True God; begotten, not made; of one essence with the Father, by Whom all things were made;
Who for us men and for our salvation came down from Heaven, and was incarnate of the Holy Spirit and the Virgin Mary, and became man.
And He was crucified for us under Pontius Pilate, and suffered, and was buried.
And the third day He arose again, according to the Scriptures, and ascended into Heaven, and sits at the right hand of the Father;
and He shall come again with glory to judge the living and the dead; Whose Kingdom shall have no end. And in the Holy Spirit, the Lord, the Giver of Life, Who proceeds from the Father;
Who with the Father and the Son together is worshipped and glorified; Who spoke by the prophets. And in One, Holy, Catholic, and Apostolic Church. I acknowledge one baptism for the remission of sins.
I look for the resurrection of the dead, and the life of the world to come.

As you can see, the wording has changed through the years.

Writings and Teachings

I asked Augustine what he wrote of the Nicene Creed.

I supported the words of the Nicene Creed. When I lived, I based my writings on the information that was available. It was not until I returned home that I realized some of what I wrote was in error.

Many of the individuals that were chosen to speak the words of God were also given the gift to heal others as proof of their divine connection. I inquired if in his lifetime as Augustine he performed any miracles.

Yes; I was given the gift of healing, just as you are given that gift. I healed many people, but few of my actions were recorded.

"What did you teach of abortion?"

As my past became clear, I realized that the taking of life while still in the womb was not the teachings of God and was an unforgivable sin.

Saint Augustine – Philippe de Champaigne – cc1647 – Los Angeles County Museum of Art, Los Angeles, CA.

"What is your opinion of the widespread abortion practices we see in our modern culture?"

I am sickened by what I see today. That is part of the growing strength of Satan; it must change, as much other evil must change.

"What did you teach about Creation?"

I taught that God created man and woman.

Constantine wrote of original sin, or the concept that the origin of sin dates to the first man, Adam, who disobeyed God by eating the forbidden fruit and transferred his sin and guilt to his descendants, or all humans. When I asked Augustine if his opinion on original sin had changed since the time of his writing, he answered:

Yes; the cause of original sin is free will. Free will can be used for good, or it can be used for evil.

In his writings he expressed a belief in double predestination, or the belief that God chooses some people for damnation and others for salvation. When I asked Augustine if he changed his opinion on that subject, the response was:

I did, but that was wrong. God only prepares people or souls to enter free of sin. There is no predetermination of evil.

"What was your opinion about women?"

I always thought man and woman were equals.

"When do you consider that the killing associated with war is acceptable?"

You must always protect yourselves. Fighting in the name of self-preservation is acceptable.

"What was your opinion of the Jewish faith?"

When I lived, I thought the Jewish faith was a pathway to heaven. Today it is an acceptable faith, but in some ways, it has gone astray.

As I mentioned earlier, the writings of Augustine laid much of the foundation for the teachings of the Catholic Church. My guess is that his assumption of celibacy played a large role in the decree that priests remain celibate so they are closer to God. I asked the Saint what he thought of the practice of the current Catholic Church. He responded:

The current Catholic Church has strayed from the teachings of God. I am sickened by what priests have done to children; they have committed an unforgivable sin and will pay when they return over here.

I hope they enjoy the lower level when they return to heaven. As Augustine grew older, his writings reflected some changes in his early opinions. I asked who he considered the greatest influence in his writings.

I studied all of the great philosophers and writings of the day. As I grew older, I acquired the ability to communicate with my guides; they led me to change much of my thinking. I tried to write extensively about my confessions and mistakes.

While in Heaven

Some of his work expanded on the works of Saint Paul the Apostle. I inquired what role Saint Paul plays in his work while in heaven. He replied:

He and I are very close over here. Paul wrote much about the one God and forgiveness. He and I try to bring that message to humans.

"What is your role when your soul is in heaven?"

I try to bring the words of our Lord to individuals such as you and Connie. I will continue to offer you guidance and help with your writing. Your books are very important to our goals of bringing truth and love to all.

I can vouch for the fact that he has been an incredible force in my writing. I inquired if he had ever reincarnated since he walked the earth as Augustine.

No; I serve my Lord from this side.

I would comment that he is doing an admirable job. As we ended the Facebook Live session, I asked if he had a final message for those listening to his words.

Yes; I want to confirm that what I tell you is the words of our Lord. To those of you listening tonight, I want you to have no doubts that Barry and Connie speak the words of our Lord. We will continue to provide information and guidance for all. We are at the beginning of a long journey. Evil must be defeated! With that message, I will leave you tonight, but know that I am available for guidance if you pray to me and ask. God bless all of you watching tonight, amen!

He ended by informing all that there is guidance available for all who believe and ask for it. I would strongly advise that you take him up on his offer; I know that I pray to him every night. His help and guidance have been invaluable to Connie and me.

CHAPTER 17

Mother Teresa

Mother Teresa – Charles Fagan – Knights of Collumbus.

Mother Teresa was born Agnes Gonxha Bojaxhiu on August 27, 1910, in what is now Macedonia but was at that time part of the Ottoman Empire. At the age of 18, she joined the Sisters of Our Lady of Loreto, a Catholic order that ministered to the homeless and poor in India, where she took the name Mother Teresa. In 1950, she founded the Missionaries of Charity, an order devoted to caring for the poor and the sick. That order now has branches in more than 100 cities around the world. Mother Teresa spent her life working in the slums of Calcutta, India. In 1979, she was awarded the Nobel Peace Prize, and in 1985 the Medal of Freedom from the United States. She passed on September 5, 1997, at the age of 87. In 2015, she was beatified by Pope Francis as Blessed Teresa of Calcutta and joined a place among the Catholic saints.

We had been blessed in earlier channeling sessions by her spirit and learned that she is one of Connie's guides and they work together when she is on the other side. The first time she came in for Connie, we asked her by what name she would like us to call her, and she replied:

> *You can call me Agnes.*

It is very nice to be on a first-name basis with someone with the status of Mother Teresa.

A Live Radio Appearance

At the time of writing this chapter, Connie and I are making monthly appearances on the Michael T. Vara show *Late Night in the Midlands*, where we do live channeling and take calls with questions. In August 2018, I asked Agnes if she would appear on the show with us and answer callers' questions. I explained to her that there would be a large number of skeptics and asked if she would have a message for them. Here is her message from that show:

> *I am here to bring you a message from our Lord. I know that there are skeptics out there who would never believe of my spirit presence. For those people, I want to say that I was among the poorest people in the world, and I tried my best to help them, but it was a very difficult time. Tonight is very special, in that all can hear of my advice. With that, I will take your questions.*

She then answered questions from listeners. Just imagine being one of the lucky callers that had the privilege of having their questions answered by the famous Saint.

Interview with Mother Teresa

In September of 2018, she returned to us for a longer interview on Facebook Live. Here is her message from that interview:

> *I have been waiting for this opportunity to once again speak the words of my Lord. He is here with us tonight and listening to what I am about to say. I want all of you to know that my life was spent attempting to help the poor and needy. There*

were times that even I had doubts, but my faith in God prevailed, and I was able to assist many people in my lifetime.

The members of my order have grown by the thousands, and today they help many around the world. What I accomplished is an example of what you can accomplish. This group was sent to spread the name and words of our Lord; you are capable of accomplishing what I was able to accomplish.

Never feel that you are alone; God is always with you and aware of your struggles. Tonight, I will answer many questions, and from those answers, hopefully you will gain some understanding of what I went through when I walked the earth. Today there is even more need for spreading the words of love that were spoken by our Lord. It is very upsetting to see the growth of evil and watch the results tear apart communities and families. If the hatred is not stopped, there will be no advance of humans on Earth. Hatred will be the downfall of human evolution! Satan is smiling as his powers grow and fewer and fewer speak the words of our Lord.

Barry and Connie were sent back to speak his words, and there is a book that details the events in the life of our Lord when he walked the earth. That book will become the foundation upon which your teachings will be built. Soon all of you must decide if you want to dedicate your life and time to stopping Satan; it will not be easy! In fact, it will be very difficult, but under the guidance of God, all is possible. Just remember that you were sent back for a specific mission, and all need to follow their paths. God watches over all! Never, ever forget that! God also has an undying love for all; never, ever forget that as well! I know from my personal experience how difficult it is to never wander from your path. I have and regret it. Tonight, you will learn much about me; you will learn that I was a very human person but that I truly loved my God. Keep the love of God in your hearts, and all is possible. With that statement, I will now answer some questions.

Mother Teresa lived a complex life among the poorest and most needy individuals on Earth. I started the interview by asking how she would like me to refer to her.

You may simply call me Teresa. I've already told Connie that she can refer to me as Agnes.

In earlier sessions, we had learned that she and Connie had a close soul relationship, and the Saint had told Connie that she could refer to her by her given name, Agnes.

Speaking of Heaven

In life, Teresa spoke of the wonders of heaven. I asked if she would describe heaven for our listeners.

It is impossible to explain the grandeur of heaven. Even I, who spoke of heaven every day, had no idea just how wonderful a place it is. No one can conceive of the wonders that we behold on this side every day. Do not fear death; death will be the beginning of an incredibly exciting journey for you over here. Love God, and know that your place in heaven is secure.

In previous sessions, we have discussed the realms of heaven. Our focus was always the upper and lower realms. I asked her if she would describe the middle realms, the ones where most of the souls reside, and tell us about the differences.

Most individuals occupy the middle realms. They have lived good lives, but they also made mistakes that hindered their progress. In those realms, you will be with family members, and you will be in surroundings that are familiar. Many are satisfied with life in the middle realms. Many, such as you and Connie, have chosen to advance to the highest realm. The higher you advance, the more miraculous the things you will see and be able to do.

"Can a soul visit the realms that are lower than the ones that they obtained?"

Yes; you can always visit the realms that are beneath you, but you cannot visit the realms that are above you.

"When your soul passes, is there really a light that your soul heads toward?"

There may be a light if you expect one, or you may just simply advance into heaven and be greeted by your family members.

We have been told many times that when your soul arrives in heaven, there is a review of how you led the incarnate life, and your soul is judged accordingly. I inquired how your soul is judged when it arrives in heaven.

You will first judge the events that took place in your life yourself. You are expected to know what you did wrong and what you did right. Your guides will work with you to have you understand your mistakes so they are not repeated.

What you do in an incarnate lifetime definitely influences what happens when you get on the other side. As we all look back at some of the events in our life, we should all be thankful that we have such a forgiving God.

A Long Soul History

For a soul to be as advanced as Teresa's, she would have served God in many previous lifetimes. I started by inquiring if she had ever served God on other planets.

Of course, as all of you did. I served thousands of lifetimes on other planets.

That is a bunch of lifetimes away from Earth! I asked what it was like to serve God on other planets.

Some planets follow the teachings of God. Some, such as Earth, are young cultures and are trying to advance toward being godlike. It is not easy to be a young culture.

One of these days, humans will realize that they are not the most important beings in the universe, simply a young and struggling culture with much to learn. Many of the souls that walked the earth with Jesus were part of his soul family. I inquired if she knew Jesus in life.

Yes, I was a close follower of Jesus.

"What was your role in that lifetime?"

I followed our Lord but was not part of his inner group. At times I traveled with the group and always tried to bring others to our Lord.

As is the case with the other holy spirits that have come to us, Teresa is a close member of God's soul family and served him in many lifetimes. My next question was if she ever reincarnated between the lifetime when she walked the earth with Jesus and her incarnate life as Teresa.

Yes; I returned in the Middle Ages and was a high-ranking monk in the Catholic Church.

"What year were you born in that lifetime?"

890.

"So you returned in the ninth century?"

Yes.

"Can you tell us about that life?"

During those years, the Catholic Church controlled all Christian thinking. I actually played a role in revising some of the gospels; it was a difficult time. There was much bloodshed as the Roman Catholic Church fought for its existence.

Her soul decided to return during the depths of the Dark Ages. This was a time of bloodshed, little law, and much brutality. The soul energy of Teresa can never be accused of returning to a time of luxury. In earlier sessions, we had learned that her soul and that of Connie's had an interesting interaction. I asked her if she had a soul relationship with my wife. She replied:

Yes; she and I work together when we are both on the other side. We have lived together many times in the service of God.

We were told that Connie and I have been together six or seven lifetimes. I asked Teresa how many times she and Connie had been together.

Many, perhaps hundreds.

It is a good thing I am not a jealous person. "Would you like to say anything about her soul?"

Yes; her soul is advanced to the highest level, as is yours. She returns to the commands of God; that is why you and she are upon Earth today.

Life as Teresa

We are all aware of her amazing soul journey as Mother Teresa. I asked Teresa what led her to a life of service. She replied:

My guides informed me of my path, and I tried to do the best I could.

"What led you to a life helping the poor and suffering? There were many ways you could have served God."

No one was filling that role. That is why I was sent back.

As you can see, God attempts to influence the advancement of humans by directing members of his soul family to lives where they are needed. I read some articles that questioned her motives in how she lived her life. My next question addressed her purpose for helping the poor.

I wanted to help them improve their lives, but I also wanted to help improve and to advance the Catholic Church.

"Why did you choose Calcutta?"

It was the poorest place I could think of.

It is also written that there were times that she became frustrated by the extent of the suffering and questioned why God would allow such hardships to take place. Apparently, there were times that she even doubted the presence of God. I asked if she ever considered quitting helping the poor.

Yes; the job at times seemed so overwhelming. There were times that I doubted I was making any real progress. Every time I doubted my mission, God came to me and reinforced my belief and that I was on the proper path.

"In your life as Teresa, did you have the ability to receive messages from God?"

Yes; I had what you refer to as psychic abilities. I could meditate and hear his messages; those messages are what directed my life.

My guess is she never paid much attention to Leviticus and the part where psychic abilities are described as witchcraft.

It is also written that she paid more attention to the advancement of the Catholic Church than helping others. When I asked her if that was true, she answered:

Sometimes I would concentrate on growing the size of my order, but I always had the care of the poor in mind.

"In life, did you ever perform any miracles?"

No; I tried to heal others as best I could but personally never performed a miracle.

"Why did you feel chastity was required to serve God?"

I felt that the writings of the early church indicated that chastity and suffering were required to truly follow God. I now know that is not required.

For the first thousand years of the Catholic Church, priests were allowed to marry. It was only after women began to have too much influence in the church that chastity was decreed for the clergy. That order effectively reduced the influence of women.

"Was there ever a time in your life that you doubted the existence of God?"

Unfortunately, yes. I would view the incredible suffering of the poor in Calcutta and would ask myself how a loving God would ever permit such suffering to take place. I now understand that suffering of the poor is a chosen life path for the purpose of learning, so the soul can advance. Sometimes such suffering is karma for evil in a past life.

"Was there ever a time you considered yourself an agnostic?"

No; I had doubts, but I never doubted the existence of God. That is to say, my doubts never advanced to the point I felt there was no God.

"What brought you back to God when you were having these doubts?"

He would come to me in dreams and assure me of his love. Those messages were what I needed to confirm my faith.

"Did you ever, in life, preach anything that you now know is in error?"

Yes, I taught that evil souls would go to hell. There is no hell, but there is a lower level where evil souls are sent. I also taught that Jesus died for the sins of man. I now know that that was not the reason he died on the cross. He died on the cross so that humans would remember his sacrifice and, in turn, his words.

"Is there anything that you regret about your life as Teresa?"

Yes; I regret I had those moments of doubt. Those of you listening tonight, know that God is very real, and never doubt his presence!

I think the important message here is that having doubts about the presence of God is normal, and even an incredible soul such as Teresa shared those emotions. The most important lesson is that her faith overcame her doubts. Hopefully, all of us can learn from the words of Mother Teresa.

Opinions about Current Events

She readily admits that one of the main objectives in her life was to advance the Catholic Church. I asked her to voice an opinion about the current Catholic Church.

Regretfully, the current church has lost its way; the abuse of the young was condoned at the highest level. Much must change in the current church. It must rebuild and follow the true teachings of God and minister love and faith to the young, not abuse!

"What is your opinion of the current pope?"

He inherited huge problems and, in many instances, has not responded appropriately.

"What will happened to the current pope?"

He will be forced to step down. That will happen in the near future.

This reinforced what we had been told in previous sessions.
When I wrote this chapter, events in our government had reached an incredible level of hatred. I asked her opinion of what was happening in our government today.

The divisiveness sickens me, as it sickens our Lord. It will not be until your government can respect one another and worry more about serving the people and not personal power, the sooner humans can advance in your country.

President Donald Trump is one of the most controversial leaders of our country to govern. I inquired about her opinion of our current president.

He is not perfect, but he is attempting to do the best for the American people. Many hate him, and I would point out that hate is a sin.

"What do you consider the greatest evil in the world today?"

The teaching of false prophets that attempt to undermine the love of God. The false prophets lead large groups of people toward not following our Lord.

The growth of secularism and atheism is certainly leading people away from the love of God. We are told continuously about the growth of Satan. I asked her what she considered the most important message for humans. Her reply was this:

Simply to have the love of God in your heart and follow his guidance of love for one another. If all follow those words, Satan will be destroyed.

"Do you believe that humans will be able to defeat Satan?"

It will be very difficult; for the time being, the power of Satan is growing. If each person hearing me tonight promises to show love and compassion to others, that will grow, and more and more people will learn the power of love. Without love and compassion, human evolution will fail.

If the love and compassion shown by our current politicians is the example for the rest of us, humans have a lot of problems ahead. It is a reoccurring theme in all our sessions that we must show love toward our fellow humans and unite to defeat the growing influence of Satan.

Being Close to God in Heaven

The soul energy of Teresa resides in the highest realm of heaven, close to the eternal energy of Jesus. I asked her what it was like to be close to Jesus in heaven.

It is to know pure love and compassion. When you are in his presence, you understand the full power of God. It is impossible to describe until you have lived the event of being near him. While you are on Earth, your soul can find peace by having the love of God in your heart. It will not be until you come home that you find total love and peace, when you are without a physical body.

Being close to Jesus is the incentive for trying to earn access to the highest level in heaven through multiple reincarnations. I inquired if she had any plans to return to an incarnate body anytime soon.

Possibly; I will return when our Lord asks me to return. I know there are things that Connie and I must do when she returns home, but there will be a time when my and her souls will again walk the earth.

"What is your current role in heaven?"

My current role is to help humans to care for the needy and the poor. I try to guide human souls. There are many good souls walking the earth, and they need to step forward and understand that there is no greater calling than to help the needy and the suffering.

We have been told that there are times when multiple lifetimes are planned in advance. I asked if she had any idea of what her future lifetimes would be like. Her answer was this:

No, there is much to do before I return; my life plan has not, as of yet, been prepared.

Her soul is very busy helping others and leading them back to the love of God, whether in incarnate body or soul energy in heaven.

Messages from Mother Teresa

All of the interviews in this book were given in Facebook Live sessions for our group, Words of God Then and Now. I asked Teresa if she had a specific message for members of our group. She replied:

Yes; you have been chosen to spread the words of God as delivered by Barry and Connie. I can assure you that if you follow the teachings that you hear from them, your soul will advance in the realms of heaven.

"Has your soul ever worked with any of the souls of members of this group in prior lives?"

Yes; I have known many of you before. There will be a time when you come home that I will greet you as you enter heaven. Know that you were sent back for a reason.

"Do you have a message for Connie and myself?"

Yes; you must continue as you are. We will support you in your mission. It is also important that you find others with the ability to communicate with us. There will be a time that you and Connie will return home and others must carry on. You have all been chosen for this very important mission; keep the love of God in your heart. You cannot fail!

There is no doubt that with all the hatred in the world today, bringing the love of God to many will take a long-term plan that will outlive both Connie and myself. Others must step forward to carry the message to those willing to open their hearts to the words and love of God. I inquired if she had a final message for us.

I want to thank all of you for listening to my words here tonight. Jesus is here and will now give you a short message.

We had been told that Jesus would be listening and would bless us with a message.

Message of Jesus

> *I want to thank all of you for the beginnings that you are now taking to spread my words. I love each and every one of you! You must grow strong, knowing that I am with each and every one of you at all times. Together we will conquer Satan. I will not let you fail in this! Soon much will take place, and it will be much easier for you to bring others to my words at that time. Prepare yourselves for what is to come! Know that you are participating in a miracle. God bless each and every one of you here tonight! Amen!*

In life, Mother Teresa had a diminutive frame, with the soul of a giant. Her appearance was truly a blessed miracle for all of us.

CHAPTER 18

Billy Graham, a Son of Jesus

In February of 2018, the Reverend Billy Graham died at his home in Montreat, North Carolina, at the age of 99 after a long battle with Parkinson's disease. He was known as one of the greatest evangelistic preachers of all time, and during his lifetime, his words reached over 200 million persons. He conducted more than 400 crusades and held evangelistic rallies in more that 185 countries and territories. He authored 34 books. In life, he was known as the "preacher of the presidents," having prayed with five American presidents.

Reverend Billy Graham – Yousuf Karsh – Smithsonian, Washington DC.

In life, preaching as an evangelist, he taught that the Bible was the infallible word of God and that Jesus died on the cross to save the souls of man, and those not saved would go to hell. He also taught that Jesus would return in the end of days to rescue the faithful. In our channeling sessions, we have learned that some of his teachings and the words written in the Bible are distortions of the true teaching of our Lord.

In September of 2018, we were blessed with his spirit presence, and we conducted an interview with the famous evangelist on Facebook Live. He began the session with the following message:

Yes, I am here tonight to once again speak the words of God. It has been a while since my words were spoken to many people. Tonight is very special. I want to start tonight by saying that I am very appreciative of the opportunity to speak to all of you. In my life, I spoke many words of God, and those words were heard by millions of people. Tonight, I know, the crowd is much smaller but very, very important. God has selected many of you to fulfill a mission of spreading his words of love and trying to stop the spread and effects of Satan. Satan is very real in your lives and is gaining strength. Only spreading the true words of God will slow the advance of Satan; together we will be successful. Barry and Connie are bringing you the true words of God. They were sent back for this specific mission. What they tell you is the actual truth. I will try to amplify on their words and explain many things here tonight. I helped Barry make up many questions that he will ask tonight. Many are controversial, but I intend to answer them truthfully, as I attempted to answer all things truthfully while in life. Just know that you are the chosen ones. Go forth and spread the words of God, and you will find your rewards with me in heaven. Jesus is very aware of what we are doing here tonight. This is my first real attempt to spread his words since arriving on this side. God will bless all of you as he has blessed me. I will now begin to answer the questions.

I started the interview by asking him how he would prefer that I address him.

You can call me Brother, but the rest can refer to me as Reverend Graham.

It is certainly an honor to refer to such a remarkable soul as "Brother."

Speaking of Heaven

In life, he spoke of the wonders of heaven. I asked if he would tell us what heaven was really like now that he was on the other side.

It is beyond description! It is the most magnificent place. All things are possible here. Those that have spoken of our God are in realms where all is possible. Those that have not spoken nor believed in him are in lower realms and are not having the experiences of the upper realms.

When the soul first arrives in heaven, it is greeted by family and other souls. I asked Reverend Graham who was there to greet him when he finally arrived home. He replied:

When I crossed over, Jesus was waiting for me, as well as my mother and many of the holy spirits that you have conversed with.

That must have been quite a welcoming! For Jesus and the other holy spirits to have greeted him, his soul must have been very advanced.

"What would you tell us about the realms of heaven?"

There are seven realms or levels in heaven; your soul has to experience all possible and share a true love of God to progress in those realms. God is in the seventh realm, as are many of the holiest of souls.

He confirmed what we have been told previously in channeling sessions.

Prior Service to God

In our conversations with other holy spirits, we found out that they had served our Lord many times in prior lives to attain their elevated status in heaven. I asked if he had ever served our Lord in other prior lives.

I served our God in many, many lifetimes prior to the one as Billy Graham.

"Did you ever serve God on other planets in your prior lives?"

Of course, as did all of you. Humans have not walked the earth nearly as long as your soul energies have existed; therefore, all of you have served our God on other planets.

That is exactly what we have heard from other holy spirits. I inquired if in one of his prior lives, he walked the earth at the same time as Jesus walked the earth. He answered:

Yes, I was blessed to have lived at the same time as our Lord; he was my father, and I was his son. In your book, you will tell all of the truths concerning the actual life of our Lord. As you are well aware, there were four other brothers and sisters that were members of our family. You were also there as well; that is why you have such a personal relationship with our Lord. He watches closely over you and Connie and leads and advises you as you spread the words of God

In my previous book, *Spirits Speak: Channeling the Life of Jesus*, I devoted a chapter to the married life of Jesus, so I will not go into the details of his married life. Billy Graham was a reincarnated son of Jesus and was sent back to spread the words of God. I decided to ask a question that would guarantee that I was speaking to a reincarnated son of our Lord. I asked him to tell me the name of his mother in that lifetime. He responded:

As you are aware, our mother's name was Toba. She is with me here in heaven and watches over you and Connie as well.

He confirmed the name of the wife of Jesus. I asked if, in that lifetime, he knew John the Baptist.

Yes, John was our friend and stayed with us many times; he was a wonderful person in life. A lot of fun and good humor. He loved the family of our Lord.

"Would you like to give us more details of that prior life?"

Much of those details will be in your next book; just suffice at this time to say that our soul history has been deeply intertwined.

It is interesting to note that they already have my next book planned for me. They just have not told me what it will be.

Serving in Heaven

The fact that he was speaking to us tonight was proof that he was still serving our Lord in heaven. I inquired what his current role is in heaven.

My role is to continue spreading the words of God. I will try my best to influence others and show them the path to the all-knowing and loving God.

As the son of Jesus in a prior life, he had a very unique relationship with Jesus. I asked him if he ever had the opportunity in his lifetime with Jesus to discuss reincarnation. He answered:

No; he left us at a relatively young age to begin his mission. Once he left, I never saw him in life again. I now see him on a regular basis.

Just imagine the miracle of being able to see Jesus on a regular basis! I asked Reverend Graham if he was planning to reincarnate anytime soon.

That is a decision up to our Lord. When he decides that it is time for me to return, I will return.

He is a true servant of God on both sides of the veil! In his life as Billy Graham, he preached a strict evangelistic interpretation of the Bible.

Not Quite Accurate

Some of his teachings contrast with what we have been told during our channeling sessions. My next question addressed what his opinion of reincarnation was in his lifetime as Billy Graham.

I did not accept the concept of reincarnation. I believed that your soul lived a single lifetime and either went to heaven or to hell.

"What is your current view of reincarnation now that you are on the other side?"

Obviously, it has changed. Now that I am here, it is very apparent that reincarnation is the basis of how your soul progresses.

"You preached that the Bible was the infallible word of God. Now that you are on the other side, do you still believe it?"

No; now that I am with our Lord, I can see how man has manipulated his words so that they can have more power.

Evangelical Christians are very critical of our work, many telling me that conversing with spirits is demonic and any criticism of the words of the Bible is an unforgivable sin. I asked the Reverend Graham what he would now say to Evangelical Christians who believe that every word in the Bible is true.

I would say to them that they should open their minds and try to understand that there are parts of the Bible that reflect my father's words, but there are also parts that are incorrect. I know that is a very difficult concept, and in life I would have rejected it. The act of dying opens one's mind.

"When Evangelical Christians arrive at the other side, will they have trouble accepting the truth?"

Yes, at first I had trouble accepting the realities of my father's true teachings. I quickly learned that all of what I spoke in life was not correct; much was, especially the part of finding the love of God.

It is sad that people that truly believe in God and want to go to heaven are told to base their belief on a document that has been altered by man through the years. No one took notes as Jesus spoke, and the earliest writings took place two generations after his death, and they were based on stories based on the memories of those who heard him. They will be rewarded for the way they led their lives but will find their belief path was flawed.

The Billy Graham Evangelistic Association teaches that Jesus came for one reason: to bring us back to God. He did this by becoming the final sacrifice for our sins through his death on the cross. I asked if he still thought that Jesus died on the cross to save the souls of man. His reply was this:

No, I now know that he died on the cross so that he would be remembered.

One basic tenet of the Christian Church is that there will be a Second Coming of Christ, and that will be the event when evil is defeated and our Lord will establish his reign of justice and peace. I stated that Reverend Graham during his life spoke that there would be a time when Jesus would return, so I asked, now that he is on the other side, does he still believe it?

Jesus will never return. It is possible that God will decide to return in another form, but the form of Jesus will not return.

One of the fearsome predictions in the book of Revelation concerns the end of days. I inquired what he thought of that gospel. He was quite emphatic in his answer.

The book of Revelation was influenced by Satan! That book is totally wrong. There will be no end of days! If humans cease to exist, it will be because of their own actions.

We were told that in different interviews. I inquired what words of the Bible he considered the most distant from the teachings of our Lord.

I believe that preaching the fear of God and the act of fearing him are some of the greatest errors in the Bible. God is love, not fear, and there is no hell.

In life, Reverend Graham spoke about the ravages of hell as a penalty for not accepting God. Since he brought up the subject of hell, I asked what he taught about it.

I followed the words in the Bible and spoke of the fires of hell. I now know that hell does not exist in that form; however, there is a lower realm of nothingness that would be similar to hell.

"Did you preach that those that did not believe in God could not be saved?"

I preached that the love of God was vital to salvation. I now know it is possible to live a good life without believing in God and that the nonbelievers will be forgiven.

My guess is that was a very difficult lesson to learn on the other side.

Presidentially Speaking

Reverend Graham was known as the preacher of the presidents, having prayed with five different leaders of our country. I asked him which president he felt was closest to God.

I thought that Lyndon Johnson was closest to God. I was very upset when I learned the truth of his life.

Knowing that Lyndon Johnson was responsible for the assassination of John Kennedy and that in life Reverend Graham was very close to Johnson, I asked him what he thought of him now that he was on the other side.

He has been sent to the lowest level for all the terrible things he did in life. He was responsible for the death of President Kennedy; for that he will pay dearly.

Harry Truman did not speak kindly of Reverend Graham, accusing him of wanting publicity. I inquired if, now that he was on the other side, he got along with the former president. He replied:

Yes; Harry and I have resolved our differences.

Dying does tend to resolve differences. My next inquiry concerned his opinion of President Obama.

He was not what he appeared. I would like to say no more about that.

Sometimes discretion is the better part of valor.

Opinions

Reverend Graham grew up during the Depression in North Carolina. It is said that in his early life he had some controversial beliefs. I started on this subject by asking if he was ever anti-Semitic.

Unfortunately, in my youth, I did have anti-Semitic thoughts; as I grew older, I put them behind me.

"Were you ever homophobic?"

Unfortunately, once again, I did have those thoughts.

"What is your current opinion on homosexuality?"

I personally do not think it is natural. The individuals are judged by how they live their lives and their love of God.

In the 1930s and '40s, rural North Carolina was not the most hospitable place to preach racial equality. I asked his opinion on segregation during his early years.

I felt that segregation was wrong, but I was influenced by the people around me. I did not do as much as I should have concerning segregation.

"What was your opinion about Martin Luther King?"

I did not believe he was a true leader. I now understand differently.

Reverend Graham had a very interesting opinion about women. He did not allow his daughters to have a college education. I asked him about his opinion concerning women.

I tried to keep women as they were mentioned in the Bible. I always thought they were equals, but in many ways, I did not act like that.

"Why did you not allow your daughters to be educated for a career?"

I thought the place of a woman was in the home with a husband. I considered educating women as being disruptive to a happy home life.

"What is your opinion of the Catholic Church?"

I am saddened about what the church has become. They have not protected the young from abuse, and they will pay the price. I love the Catholic people that share my love of God.

"What is your opinion of the current pope?"

He is not doing what needs to be done to save the Catholic Church. He has protected those that abused the young.

"What will be the fate of the current pope?"

He will soon step down.

We have been told that before, and I've had it as a prediction on my website since the current pope was chosen. I asked Reverend Graham why there is such a divide between Evangelicals and Catholics. His reply was:

Leaders of both sides have exaggerated the difference between the two churches. It is the fault of the leaders, not the people.

"What do you think of Pastor Robert Jeffress?"

I think he is trying to take my place. If he is capable of doing that remains to be seen.

His answers to the controversial questions were very straightforward and honest. I inquired if there was anything about his lifetime as Billy Graham that he would change now that he has the understanding of being on the other side. His answer was this:

Yes; I would like to relive the early parts of my life, where I had negative thoughts about segregation, homosexuality, and the role of reincarnation. I guess being over here really points out your mistakes.

Even a person that led millions to God has things about his life that he would change. In that respect, he is no different from all of us.

Messages for All of Us

Reverend Graham was an individual almost bigger than life, and I wanted to take advantage of his words of advice. As a person that preached to more people than any other pastor in history, I asked him what he would suggest for Connie and me to do to reach more people with our messages. He replied:

Just continue as you are, building a strong nucleus of followers. Those that follow you must build their strength and knowledge so they, too, can also be effective. When the time arrives, you will reach millions.

I find it very hard to believe we can ever reach that many people with the amount of time remaining for us in this visit to Earth. I inquired if he had a personal message for Connie and me.

Yes; we watch what you do and are pleased. We know that you are doing your best. In the future, you will heal many, and that will generate confidence that you really do speak the words of God.

When I heal others, I am fully aware that it is not me but the power of God behind the healing.

My Facebook group, Words of God Then and Now, is dedicated to spreading the truth about the teachings of our Lord and bringing his contemporary messages to the people. I asked Reverend Graham what he would have the members of the group do to spread the words of God.

They must stand firm concerning their convictions regarding the love of God. Once they have no doubts, it will become easier to spread his words. It is difficult when among skeptics. We will assist each in their special message.

When I asked how he would assist the members of the group, the reply was this:

I will come to members individually in their dreams and give them advice.

"Do you have a final message for us?"

Yes; you heard much information tonight from me. I appreciate the opportunity to once again speak the words of God. Jesus is here with me tonight and wants to give the final blessing.

A Message From Jesus

We had not been told that we would also have a message from Jesus on this evening. I could feel his loving energy as we began to receive the following message:

I want all to know how proud I am of what each and every one of you is accomplishing. You now know of my love and my ability to send the holiest of spirits to you with messages. Spread the words of my love for all and that I am always with you. Your prayers are heard; have faith in God, and all will be well. God bless all of you here tonight. Spread my words as you hear them from Barry and Connie; they are truly my words. Amen

As we approached the Christmas holidays in 2018, we asked Reverend Graham to return to us for a special message. Here is that message for all of us:

Good evening. I am honored to once again have the opportunity to speak the words of our Lord God to a large group of individuals. In life I was honored to speak to the many. I did my best to bring my words of love of God to as many as possible. Tonight I want to speak of the birth of the Christ child. On that momentous day 2,000 years ago, a child was born that was going to change the world forever. His words would become the basis of a faith and a way of life based on love and charity. Now that I am on the other side, I am privileged to know our Lord and his mother, Mary—their souls are a miracle! The fact that I can speak to you tonight is a miracle! Know that my words are real, and know that what I tell you is the good word. God came to earth as Jesus, and so do his words continue to ring throughout the world. The celebration of the birth of our Lord is a sacred moment. We celebrate it each year, and it is a time for devotion to family and to rededication of one's life to preaching the love of God. It is that love of God that will guide you when you return home under the realms of heaven. Know the truth of the good word. Know that God is with you each and every day; know that he will watch over you as you celebrate his birth and as you lead your lives. Know as well that love is the answer; know that spreading that love to others will help defeat Satan and the evil that abounds on Earth today. As we celebrate the season, dwell upon the message of our Lord and not upon the commercial aspects of the holiday. Christ is the reason for Christmas! There is no other reason; without the birth of Christ, there would be no Christmas! Know well what I tell you tonight: go forth and know that God is a universal energy that watches over all. He will be with you; he will attempt to guide you, and with these words, I would like to wish you all a Merry and a God-like Christmas! Good night!

The soul that walked the earth as Billy Graham has a long history of serving our Lord, and there is every indication that he will continue to be his servant in heaven and future incarnate lives. We have been truly blessed with his spirit presence and words.

CHAPTER 19

Conclusion

Every day, the holiest of spirits attempt to communicate their messages of love and faith to each of us. Often, that communication is facilitated by our spirit guides. Unfortunately, most of us ignore or are not aware of these messages. It took over 60 years for me to realize what was taking place, and that was with a lot of effort from the spirits around me. I am living proof that it is never too late for an individual to learn how to communicate with and become closer to God.

In this book, I have attempted to bring you the messages as we received them, not only from Jesus but from the spirits of his disciples and holy spirits that served him when he walked the earth and in subsequent lifetimes. You learned that Mother Teresa and Billy Graham were reincarnated souls that walked with Jesus. Certain souls have served God in many past lifetimes and are selected to return to incarnate lives in an effort to influence the free will of humans. In many instances, the messages differ from the classical content of the Bible. In many instances, they support what is written in the gospels. What is required is an open mind to sort out what makes sense and what does not.

What we have presented to the readers of this book is a scenario of the messages of Jesus and the holy spirits that is believable, stripped of the exaggerations that have been added for thousands of years to give control to the leaders of organized religions. Their messages of love and faith are very simple and compelling. Jesus lived a normal lifetime while on Earth, complete with a wife and children. It was only in the last three years of his life that he carried out his ministry and changed the world. His handful of devout followers and disciples continued to speak his words and began the greatest movement to affect human development: Christianity. It was all part of a preordained plan by God. It is their desire that we carry on their tradition and spread the true words and messages of the universal energy we refer to as God, Spirit, or whatever name you prefer.

You have learned much about the lives and personalities of the group of individuals that spread his words throughout the civilized world that existed 2,000 years ago. Many of these young men and women left their families with the almost certain knowledge that their lives would end painfully. They realized that speaking of the one God was in stark contrast to the beliefs of the powerful Roman Empire. Jesus told them that they would join him in heaven, and they had no doubts as they spread his words. As a reward for their continued service to God, their souls reside in the upper realm of heaven, where they continue to teach of the love of the all-powerful Deity. The message remains much the same today in view of the growing presence of evil in our modern world. The presence of weapons of mass destruction makes the need to spread his words of love even more critical if man is to continue to evolve.

In this book, the reader was introduced to the concept of everlasting life through multiple reincarnations of the energy of the soul. This concept is in direct conflict with the classic belief that your soul gets a single lifetime to determine if it goes to heaven or hell. In fact, your soul energy has lived many lifetimes, in which it has worked to advance in the realms of heaven. Your soul will live many lifetimes in the future as it continues to learn and become one with God.

Another stark contrast to classical biblical thought is that there is no hell, at least not the famous one with fire, brimstone, and a guy with a pitchfork running around in a red suit. We are told there is a lower level in heaven where the bad guys are sent, but it is a place of nothingness. The soul can remain there for a long time until it decides to change its ways and God allows it to get out. When it is allowed to come out of the lower level, the soul will have to repay what it has done in future lifetimes. There really is such a thing as bad karma.

Perhaps the greatest departure from classical teachings is the concept that each galaxy in heaven has its own God, with different beliefs and structure. Our God presides over the Milky Way—no small feat, considering the immense number of stars and planets it encompasses. Even harder to believe is that there are intelligent planets where they completely follow his teachings. Our human culture is quite young and has a lot of learning to do if it is to continue to evolve and join the advanced civilizations. Humans are their own worst enemy through their free will and egos, acting in spite of God and the spirit guides attempting to lead us.

In many instances, I asked Jesus and the holy spirits to describe heaven for us. Many stated that it was unimaginable in its magnificence. It is a place of wonder and vivid colors. There are seven realms, and the magnificence grows greater as you obtain higher levels and you become closer to God. Your advancement is determined by how you live your lives and your learning experiences. Even the most renowned persons of faith, such as Reverend Billy Graham and Mother Teresa, state that they underestimated the wonders of heaven. You also learned that heaven is not restricted to those who confess a belief in God, but entry is based on how you live your life and your love for others. Heaven is not the property of only Christians. There are many paths to advancing in the realms of heaven, and its realms cannot be claimed by a single religion. It is even inhabited by soul energies from other planets. The possibilities are endless.

The messages and statements bring a contemporary meaning to the words and messages of God. These words were given to us so that they could be used as a guide for everyone. You were given the simplest of messages: namely, if you have the love of God in your heart, show that love to others, and live a good life, you will advance in the realms of heaven. The overriding question is how many of you will take these words to heart and follow his commands. Keep in mind that not only the future of your soul but that of the human race depends on it.

Our path bringing you the messages of the holy spirits will continue into the future. We invite you to join us in my Facebook group, Words of God Then and Now, or subscribe to my YouTube channel under the name Barry Strohm. My next book will bring you the teachings of God and more opinions of the holy spirits and even archangels. Our journey is far from over; come join us.

CPSIA information can be obtained
at www.ICGtesting.com
Printed in the USA
LVHW030617220221
679516LV00002B/98